Recipes Worth Sharing

by Tara McConnell Tesher

Author, Tara McConnell Tesher
Editors, Jodi Flayman, Merly Mesa, Carol Ginsburg
Recipe Development and Food Styling, Patty Rosenthal
Photographer and Stylist, Victoria Krog
Assistant Photographer, Kelly Rusin
Post Production, Hal Silverman of Hal Silverman Studio
Cover and Page Design, Lorraine Dan & Luise Johnson of Grand Design

The paper in this printing meets the requirements of the ANSI Standard Z39.48-1992.

While every care has been taken in compiling the recipes for this book, the publisher, Cogin, Inc., or any other person who has been involved in working on this publication assumes no responsibility or liability for any errors or omissions, inadvertent or not, that may be found in the recipes or text, nor for any problems or damages that may arise as a result of preparing these recipes.

If food allergies or dietary restrictions are a concern, it is recommended that you carefully read ingredient product labels as well as consult a nutritionist or your physician to determine if a particular recipe meets your dietary needs.

We encourage you to use caution when working with all kitchen equipment and to always follow food safety guidelines.

To purchase this book for business or promotional use or to purchase more than 50 copies at a discount, or for custom editions, please contact Cogin, Inc. at the address below.

Inquiries should be addressed to:
Cogin, Inc.
1770 NW 64 Street, Suite 500
Fort Lauderdale, FL 33309

ISBN: 978-0-9981635-5-0

Printed in the United States of America
First Edition

❖ foreword ❖

I have known and worked with Tara Tesher for more than 20 years at QVC. In addition to being long-time colleagues, we're also dear friends and neighbors. Over time, I've had the good fortune to be a guest at parties and dinners where Tara cooks and serves delicious food with ease and perfection. When it came time to write a new cookbook, it made sense that Tara would draw from the dishes and treats she has served so successfully all these years.

Recipes Worth Sharing takes Tara's lifelong love affair with food to the next level. Here, you'll find her spin on classic dishes and family favorites that are sure to please every appetite. Tara believes, as I do, that cooking should be joyful, and an expression of love. Each of her recipes is accessible, easy to make, and super satisfying. You'll never want to serve the same old dish again with these new options at your fingertips.

This book includes eight mouthwatering chapters filled with Tara's time-tested appetizers, breakfast treats, meats, soups, desserts, and oh-so-much more! With full-color photos throughout, you'll never be left wondering what the completed recipe should look like or how it should be served. You'll also love that the ingredients are easy to find in your pantry or local grocery store.

I'm thrilled with the variety in this cookbook and can't wait to try all of these yummy and tempting treats. From the Gooey Pecan Cinnamon Buns and Oven-Roasted Buffalo Wing Dings to Gail's Favorite Chicken Cacciatore and the decadent No-Bake S'mores Cake, you'll always be ready to serve a home run to party guests and family alike. Also, don't miss the Deep Dish Pizza Bake, Rancher's Picnic Potato Salad, and—my personal favorite—Tara's Famous Garlicky Guacamole!

With our lives and families busier than ever, it's important to have a great guide to wonderful recipes and easy entertaining tips. *Recipes Worth Sharing* delivers all of that and more. Take time to browse every page of this wonderful collection, and you'll find yourself quickly getting your shopping list together. Let Tara take you on a culinary journey, and one thing will happen for sure—you'll be thrilled you made the trip!

Warmly,
David Venable
QVC Host, *In the Kitchen with David*®

❖ introduction ❖

Anyone who knows me knows how passionate I am about food and entertaining. Whether I'm hosting a holiday celebration or just having a few friends over to watch a game, I love being the hostess with the "most-est"!

For me, entertaining is all about spending quality time with friends and family (and sharing lots of good food!). But I find it's kind of hard to enjoy your company if you're spending all your time cooking and cleaning in the kitchen. That's why I'm all about quick and easy menus. My cooking philosophy is inspired by the same philosophy that led me to create temp-tations®. With temp-tations, I wanted to create a set of bakeware that would allow home cooks to prep, cook, serve, and clean up, as easily as possible. The same goes for my recipes!

I also feel that everyone should be armed with a bunch of really good recipes…recipes that are tried and true. Ones that are so good that everyone who tries them will ask you for the recipes every time you make them. That's exactly why I created this cookbook. I wanted you to have more than 130 recipes that are positively worth sharing.

What sets this book apart from some of my earlier cookbooks is that this time I'm featuring some of my absolute favorite recipes. These are the recipes that I make day-in and day-out, week after week, party after party.

So join me as I start my day with The Perfect Breakfast Sandwich, great for those busy days when I'm running off to QVC, as well as the Cheese & Chives Hash Brown Waffles and Sunday Brunch Strudel that I make when I have a bit more time. You'll also discover what my husband, Ed's favorite appetizers are. If you guessed Vacation-Worthy Coconut Shrimp and Cheddar Bacon Deviled Eggs, you were right! I can't wait for you to see how I've put my own twist on lots of classic favorites. Take my Not-Your-Grandma's Chicken Pot Pie recipe, for instance—I've changed it up with a twist on the traditional top crust that's really irresistible. And don't forget to check out my Tex-Mex Chicken Stuffed Shells, an unexpected change from a typical stuffed shell recipe. And there's a whole chapter on side dishes to go with your favorite entrées.

And because a cookbook wouldn't be complete without a chapter on desserts, you can bet your sweet tooth will be satisfied. (Those of you who know me from QVC already know I am a lover of all things dessert!) From Cinnamon Apple Cobbler to Crazy Good Chocolate Cake, there's something for everyone. Don't forget the extra scoop of ice cream!

For those of you who love reading cookbooks as much as I do, I hope you enjoy reading the stories that I've provided along with every recipe. You'll also get lots of what I call "Tara's Tips," which are basically my best tips and tricks for making and presenting the best version of my recipes.

I hope you enjoy the recipes I've shared with you, and will get great pleasure from sharing them with your family and friends.

Tara

table of contents ❖

❖ dedication ❖

This cookbook is dedicated to everyone who has joined me on my journey to bring families and friends around the table ... one dish at a time.

FOOD IS THE *ingredient* that binds us **TOGETHER**

- Unknown

There is no *Joy* in possession without sharing

- Erasmus

A balanced diet is a cookie in each hand

-Barbara Johnson

There is no sincerer *Love* than the love of food

-George Bernard Shaw

THERE'S NOTHING **BETTER** THAN SHARING FOOD WITH FAMILY & FRIENDS.

– Tara McConnell Tesher

People who love to EAT are always the BEST people

- Julia Child

Vegetables ARE A MUST ON A DIET. I SUGGEST *carrot cake*, *zucchini bread*  *pumpkin pie.*

-Jim Davis

Sharing MAKES YOU BIGGER THAN YOU ARE. The more you pour out, THE MORE *life* WILL BE ABLE TO POUR IN

- Anurag Prakash Ray

THERE'S NO BETTER *compliment* THAN WHEN SOMEONE ASKS YOU FOR YOUR *recipe.*

- Tara McConnell Tesher

KITCHENS are MADE to bring families TOGETHER

- Unknown

I COOK WITH *wine.* SOMETIMES I EVEN ADD IT TO THE *food.*

-W.C. Fields

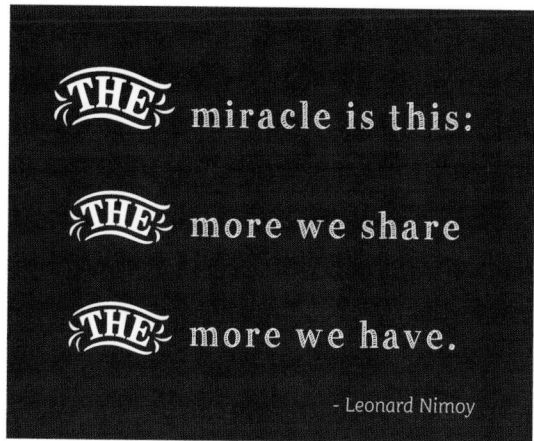

THE miracle is this:

THE more we share

THE more we have.

- Leonard Nimoy

FOOD TASTES BETTER WHEN YOU EAT IT WITH **FAMILY**

- Unknown

Share your life with others. You will have a  *Joyful life.*

- Lailah Gifty Akita

One cannot **THINK** well, **LOVE** well, **SLEEP** well, if one has not **DINED** well

-Virginia Woolf

It all starts WITH an idea & a pencil. Good thing I loved to draw as a kid.

Bountiful Breakfasts

Sunday Brunch Strudel

Everyone knows that Sundays are the best days for whipping up something for brunch. This change-of-pace, main dish strudel is a company-worthy treat that's certainly easy enough to make. It features a flaky crust and a cheesy bacon and egg filling that'll have everyone asking for more. Just set it out and let each person cut as much as they'd like.

Makes: 2   **Prep Time: 15 min**   **Cook Time: 35 min**

1 (17.25-ounce) package frozen puff pastry, thawed

4 ounces cream cheese, softened

⅓ cup milk

9 eggs, divided

¼ teaspoon salt

¼ teaspoon black pepper

1 tablespoon butter

1 cup shredded cheddar cheese

6 slices crispy cooked bacon, crumbled

❖ Preheat oven to 400 degrees F. Place each sheet of pastry dough on a 13- x 9-inch Lid-It or baking sheet and unfold; set aside.

❖ In a large bowl with an electric mixer, beat together cream cheese and milk until smooth. Add 8 eggs, the salt, and pepper, and beat until well combined. In a large skillet over medium heat, melt butter; add egg mixture and scramble until set. Remove skillet from heat and stir in cheddar cheese and bacon.

❖ With the short side of the dough towards you, spoon half of the scrambled egg mixture down center of each sheet of dough. Cut an equal number of slits, about 1 inch apart, (each about 3 inches long), on both sides of the egg mixture.

❖ In a small bowl, beat the remaining egg. Brush each strip with beaten egg and alternately crisscross strips over filling, creating a woven look. Brush top of dough with beaten egg. Repeat with second pastry dough and remaining scrambled egg mixture.

❖ Bake for 25 to 30 minutes or until golden brown. Serve immediately.

The Perfect Breakfast Sandwich

Whenever I want to treat myself for breakfast, I make an egg sandwich. It's absolutely my favorite thing. The best part is the egg; I love when the yolk dribbles over everything. If I'm not covered head-to-toe in egg yolk, I'm not truly happy with my egg sandwich. Okay, maybe not head-to-toe, but you know what I mean!

Makes: 2

Prep Time: 5 min

Cook Time: 8 min

2 tablespoons butter, divided

¼ pound sliced cooked ham (see Tip)

2 eggs

Black pepper for sprinkling

2 brioche buns

2 slices sharp cheddar cheese

¼ cup arugula (optional)

- In a large skillet over medium heat, melt 1 tablespoon butter; sauté ham for 4 to 5 minutes or until heated through. Remove to a plate and cover to keep warm.

- In the same skillet, melt remaining 1 tablespoon butter; crack eggs into pan. (Since each sandwich gets topped with just 1 egg, crack the eggs on opposite sides of the pan, so that the whites don't run into each other.) Cook for about 2 minutes, lightly sprinkle with pepper, flip eggs over, and cook until desired doneness.

- Place half of the ham on the bottom half of each bun, then top each with a slice of cheese, arugula, if desired, and an egg. Place top of each bun over egg and serve immediately.

TARA'S TIP: You can pick up the ham at the deli counter or you can do what I do, and use leftover ham. The next time you make ham for dinner, slice up the leftovers, place them in a plastic freezer bag, and pop them in the freezer. When you're ready to make your breakfast sandwiches, all you have to do is thaw and use.

Broccoli & Ham Impossible Quiche

The way I see it, there are no rules when it comes to quiche. Sometimes I make it with a crust, other times I go crustless, like with this one. As for the filling, I like to use whatever I have on hand. That might mean using up last night's leftovers, or raiding the fridge or pantry for ingredients. It's all about being creative. The combination of ham, broccoli, and cheese just happens to be one of my favorites.

Serves: 6 to 8　　　**Prep Time: 10 min**　　　**Cook Time: 25 min**

½ cup pancake and baking mix

1 teaspoon onion powder

½ teaspoon salt

¼ teaspoon black pepper

1 cup shredded Swiss cheese

1 cup shredded cheddar cheese

2 cups frozen broccoli florets, thawed

¾ cup diced ham

1 cup half-and-half

2 eggs

- Preheat oven to 400 degrees F. Coat a 9-inch pie dish with cooking spray.

- In a large bowl, combine pancake and baking mix, onion powder, salt, and pepper; mix well. Stir in the two cheeses, broccoli, and ham. Add half-and-half and mix well.

- In a small bowl, beat eggs. Add to broccoli and ham mixture, mixing well to combine. Pour into pie dish.

- Bake for 25 to 30 minutes or until a toothpick inserted in center comes out clean. Let cool for 5 minutes, then cut and serve.

TARA'S TIP: This quiche is lower in carbs than a quiche that features a traditional homemade crust. If you're interested in lightening it up even more, you can use reduced-fat cheese and load it up with even more veggies.

Bed & Breakfast Cheesecake Rollups

My mom has been making these for a long time now. She first discovered them in West Virginia, when she and my dad came to watch one of my college soccer games. They stayed at a bed and breakfast where these were served. She loved them so much, she decided to recreate them herself. The great thing is, she did it just from taste! Now our whole family loves them.

Makes: 24   Prep Time: 15 min   Cook Time: 10 min   Freeze Time: 2 hrs

1 (8-ounce) package cream cheese, softened

1 egg yolk

1 cup sugar, divided

24 slices white bread, crusts removed

1 tablespoon ground cinnamon

3 tablespoons butter, melted

In a medium bowl, beat cream cheese, egg yolk, and 1/4 cup sugar until smooth; set aside. (See Tip.)

Using a rolling pin or a clean can from your pantry, roll out each bread slice so that it's about ⅛-inch thick. Spread cream cheese mixture evenly over the bread. Roll up each slice jelly roll-style and place seam-side down on a rimmed 13- x 9-inch Lid-It or baking sheet.

In a shallow dish, combine remaining 3/4 cup sugar and the cinnamon. Brush each rollup with melted butter then roll them in the cinnamon-sugar mixture until they're completely coated. Return to Lid-It after coating. Cover and freeze for at least 2 hours, to prevent the filling from oozing during cooking.

When ready to serve, preheat oven to 400 degrees F. Bake for 10 to 12 minutes or until golden.

TARA'S TIP: You can totally get creative with your flavors here! Try adding a tablespoon of strawberry jam to make these fruity or a tablespoon of peanut butter to make them even more decadent.

Sausage & Cheese Egg Muffins

What I love the most about these is that they're so easy to make. Plus they look adorable, like mini quiches or individual-sized omelets. They pair great with other breakfast foods and can even be taken on the go if you're in a rush to get out the door. These are a hit with everyone in the family.

Makes: 6   Prep Time: 10 min   Cook Time: 25 min

8 ounces bulk breakfast sausage

7 eggs

2 tablespoons room temperature water

½ cup chopped red bell pepper

1 cup shredded pepper jack cheese

¼ teaspoon salt

¼ teaspoon black pepper

- Preheat oven to 350 degrees F. Coat a 6-cup muffin pan with cooking spray.

- In a medium skillet over medium-high heat, sauté sausage for 4 to 5 minutes or until no longer pink, stirring to break up pieces. Drain pan drippings.

- In a large bowl, whisk eggs, water, red bell pepper, cheese, salt, pepper, and crumbled sausage. Spoon mixture evenly into cups of muffin pan.

- Bake for 20 to 25 minutes or until eggs are set in center. Run a knife around edge of each to loosen and remove. Serve immediately.

TARA'S TIP: In case you're wondering why I add water rather than milk to the eggs, I find it makes them fluffier. You do want to make sure the water is room temperature and neither too hot or too cold. Cold water will toughen them, while adding anything too hot will start to cook the eggs.

Mediterranean Avocado Toast

Wherever I go, wherever they have it, I order avocado toast. I guess you could say that I'm a little bit obsessed with it. When I make it at home, I go all out. I use multigrain bread, because it's a little thicker and gives the toast more oomph, and I pair it with a poached egg because, well, it pairs so perfectly. The Mediterranean-style toppings add a really gourmet taste. I can't wait for you to try this!

Makes: 4　　　　**Prep Time: 10 min**　　　　**Cook Time: 10 min**

4 cups water

¼ cup white vinegar

4 eggs

2 ripe avocados, halved, pitted, and skin removed

1 tablespoon lemon juice

¼ teaspoon salt

4 slices whole grain bread, toasted

8 slices tomato

¼ cup crumbled feta cheese, divided

¼ cup Kalamata olives, halved, for garnish

1 tablespoon chopped red onion

Sea salt for sprinkling

Coarse black pepper for sprinkling

❖ In a medium saucepan over medium-high heat, bring water and vinegar to a boil. Reduce the heat so that the water is vigorously simmering. Crack eggs and gently drop into the water; cook for 4 to 6 minutes or until eggs are firm on the outside.

❖ Meanwhile, in a small bowl, mash avocados with a fork until desired consistency. Stir in lemon juice and ¼ teaspoon salt; set aside.

❖ Place toasted bread on a platter; spread evenly with avocado mixture and top each with 2 tomato slices. Using a slotted spoon, remove eggs from water and place 1 on each toast. Sprinkle evenly with feta cheese, olives, onion, sea salt, and coarse black pepper. Serve immediately.

Gooey Pecan Cinnamon Buns

Buying cinnamon buns can be expensive, but most people think that making them at home is too labor intensive. Well, it isn't! Supermarket shortcuts make it really easy and fun. Plus, there's something to say about having your house smell like cinnamon buns that just can't be put into words. These are so good, you might want to consider making a double batch.

Makes: 12   **Prep Time: 2 hours and 10 min**   **Cook Time: 18 min**

½ cup chopped pecans

½ cup light brown sugar

1 tablespoon
ground cinnamon

1 pound frozen bread
dough, thawed

¾ stick butter, melted

Cream Cheese Icing

3 ounces cream cheese,
softened

2 tablespoons butter,
softened

1 cup powdered sugar

1 tablespoon milk

Coat a 13- x 9-inch baking dish with cooking spray. In a small bowl, combine pecans, brown sugar, and cinnamon; set aside.

On a lightly floured surface, using a rolling pin, roll out dough into a 12- x 14-inch rectangle. (This will take a few minutes, just keep rolling gently.) Brush dough with melted butter and sprinkle evenly with brown sugar mixture. Roll up dough tightly, jelly roll-style. Cut into 12 rolls and place cut-side up in baking dish. Cover with plastic wrap and let rise in a warm part of your kitchen for about 2 hours or until doubled in size.

Preheat oven to 375 degrees F. Remove plastic wrap and bake for 18 to 20 minutes or until golden brown.

Meanwhile, in a medium bowl with an electric mixer, beat Cream Cheese Icing ingredients until smooth. Spread icing over warm rolls and serve.

Southwest-Style Breakfast Burritos

On mornings when I'm feeling really hungry, I go ahead and make myself a burrito for breakfast. Between the potatoes, peppers, eggs, and cheese, it's hard not to feel satisfied after eating one of these. And since I love Mexican food, I make mine with some of my favorite Southwest-style ingredients. You can even take these on the go if you need to.

Makes: 4   **Prep Time: 10 min**   **Cook Time: 15 min**

3 tablespoons vegetable oil

1-½ cups refrigerated cubed potatoes

1 red bell pepper, chopped

1 tablespoon butter

6 eggs, beaten

½ teaspoon salt

¼ teaspoon black pepper

1 cup shredded Mexican cheese blend

¼ cup chopped fresh cilantro

4 (10-inch) flour tortillas

½ cup guacamole

In a large skillet over medium-high heat, heat oil until hot. Sauté potatoes for 6 to 8 minutes or until they begin to brown. Add red pepper and sauté for 5 minutes or until tender; remove mixture to a bowl and set aside.

In the same skillet over medium heat, melt butter; add eggs, salt, and pepper and scramble until set. Add potato mixture, cheese, and cilantro into skillet with eggs; mix well.

Meanwhile, warm tortillas according to package directions. Spread guacamole evenly down center of each tortilla. Spoon egg mixture over guacamole. Fold bottom half of tortillas over eggs, then fold in sides and roll up. Cut in half diagonally and serve immediately.

TARA'S TIP: If you want even more Southwest flavor, add some salsa, sour cream, and hot sauce to your burritos. If these don't wake you up, nothing will!

Cheese & Chives Hash Brown Waffles

When it comes to breakfast potatoes, I'm a big fan. I'll take them any way they're served to me. When I saw that people were waffling all kinds of things, I thought—why not potatoes? These hash brown waffles are crispy, crunchy, and really tasty. Oh, and they're easy. Just mix everything together and into the waffle maker it goes. Then let the machine do the rest of the work!

Serves: 4 to 6 **Prep Time: 10 min** **Cook Time: 10 min**

1 (20-ounce) package refrigerated shredded hash browns

3 eggs, beaten

1-½ cups shredded cheddar cheese

1 tablespoon chopped chives

½ teaspoon garlic powder

¼ teaspoon paprika

½ teaspoon salt

½ teaspoon black pepper

∴ Preheat an electric waffle iron according to directions. Coat top and bottom with cooking spray.

∴ In a large bowl, combine hash browns, eggs, cheese, chives, garlic powder, paprika, salt, and pepper; mix well. Place ½-inch thick portion of hash brown mixture in waffle maker. (The amount you need for each waffle will vary based on the size of your waffle maker.) Close lid and cook for 3 to 5 minutes or until golden brown.

∴ Using a fork, remove waffle to a plate and cover with foil to keep warm. Repeat with remaining hash brown mixture. Serve hot.

TARA'S TIP: These can be made a day or two before you want to serve them. When you're ready to serve, simply reheat these on a rimmed Lid-It or baking sheet for about 20 minutes at 300 degrees F.

Grandma Gail's Overnight French Toast

This recipe is a family tradition. We've been having it on Christmas morning ever since my mom, Gail, came up with the recipe. In my family, Christmas dinner always takes place on Christmas Eve, so we prepare this at the same time. We just pop it in the fridge, leave it there overnight, and bake it on Christmas morning. By the time we're done opening presents, we garnish with a few fresh cranberries and walnuts, and breakfast is ready.

Serves: 6 to 8   Prep Time: 10 min   Cook Time: 60 min   Chill Time: overnight

1-½ sticks butter

1-½ cups brown sugar

½ cup maple syrup

⅓ cup dried cranberries

½ cup chopped walnuts, plus extra for garnish

1 large loaf French bread, cut into 1-inch slices

10 large eggs

2-½ cups milk

1-½ tablespoons vanilla extract

2 tablespoons ground cinnamon

- In a saucepan over medium heat, combine butter, brown sugar, and syrup, stirring until smooth. Bring to a boil, then pour caramelized mixture into a 13- x 9-inch baking dish. Sprinkle dried cranberries and walnuts evenly over mixture, then arrange bread slices on top.

- In a large bowl, beat eggs, milk, and vanilla. Pour mixture over bread slices, then sprinkle with cinnamon. Cover and refrigerate overnight.

- In the morning, preheat oven to 350 degrees F. Remove baking dish from refrigerator, uncover, and bring to room temperature.

- Bake for 55 to 60 minutes or until casserole is golden and set in the center. Let stand for 5 minutes before serving.

TARA'S TIP: When it comes to baking this, another option is to remove baking dish from refrigerator, uncover, and place in a cold oven. Turn oven to 350 degrees, and allow baking dish and oven to preheat together. Once it's preheated, bake as directed above.

Very Blueberry Crumb Coffee Cake

Coffee isn't important to all people, but it sure is important to me. I don't do anything before I have my first cup and I'm pretty serious about my flavored creamers. But anyway, this isn't about coffee it's about coffee cake (which funny enough, doesn't have coffee in it!). This is like having dessert for breakfast. It's sweet and crumbly and pairs perfectly with ... well, coffee!

Serves: 12 to 15   **Prep Time: 20 min**   **Cook Time: 35 min**

1 package white cake mix

6 tablespoons butter, melted

1-¼ cups quick-cooking oats, divided

2 eggs

1 (21-ounce) can blueberry pie filling

2 tablespoons butter, softened

¼ cup light brown sugar

½ cup chopped walnuts

½ teaspoon ground cinnamon

❖ Preheat oven to 350 degrees F. Coat a 13- x 9-inch baking dish with cooking spray.

❖ In a large bowl with an electric mixer, beat cake mix, 6 tablespoons melted butter, and 1 cup oats; mix until crumbly. Reserve ¾ cup of this mixture and set aside.

❖ Add eggs to remaining crumb mixture and beat until well combined; press into baking dish to create the bottom crust. Pour pie filling evenly over crust.

❖ In a medium bowl, combine reserved crumb mixture, the remaining ¼ cup oats, 2 tablespoons softened butter, the brown sugar, walnuts, and cinnamon; mix well. Sprinkle mixture evenly over filling.

❖ Bake for 35 to 40 minutes or until set and crust is golden. Let cool before cutting into squares.

Everything-in-It Granola Crackle

There's a little bit of everything in this granola—oats, nuts, seeds, and yummy dried fruit. I like keeping this with me for all the times when I find myself in between meals. I just make it ahead of time, break it into pieces, and pack it into little baggies that I can take on the go with me. Sometimes I use it in my All-in-One Smoothie Bowl (page 24) too.

Serves: 8 to 12   **Prep Time: 10 min**   **Cook Time: 45 min**

2-½ cups rolled oats

1 cup slivered almonds

¾ cup chopped walnuts

½ cup sesame seeds

½ cup roasted sunflower seeds

½ cup dried cranberries

½ cup golden raisins

½ cup honey

½ cup canola oil

2 teaspoons vanilla extract

⅔ cup light brown sugar

- Preheat oven to 350 degrees F. Line a rimmed 13- x 9-inch Lid-It or baking sheet with foil and coat lightly with cooking spray.

- In a large bowl, combine oats, almonds, walnuts, sesame seeds, sunflower seeds, cranberries, and raisins.

- In a small saucepan over low heat, combine honey, oil, vanilla, and brown sugar; bring to a boil. Remove from heat and pour over nut mixture; stir until evenly coated. Spread mixture evenly on Lid-It.

- Bake 40 to 45 minutes or until browned. While still a little warm, with a fork, break into chunks and let cool completely. Store in an airtight container.

The Fluffiest Pancakes Ever

Pancakes in my house are a family affair. I love getting everyone involved in making them, and have some great memories of doing so with my children, grandchildren, and godchildren. These pancakes are really fluffy—like really, really fluffy. And just so you know, I'm the kind of person that uses a pancake as a vehicle for butter and syrup; the more, the better.

Makes: 14　　　**Prep Time: 10 min**　　　**Cook Time: 20 min**

1-½ cups milk

¼ cup white vinegar

2 cups all-purpose flour

¼ cup sugar

1-½ teaspoons baking powder

1 teaspoon baking soda

½ teaspoon salt

2 eggs

½ stick butter, melted

1 teaspoon vanilla extract

Vegetable shortening for cooking

- In a medium bowl, stir milk and vinegar until combined; set aside for 5 minutes to allow the mixture to "sour." The milk/vinegar mixture should look curdled. (Combining these two opposites will create a delicious homemade buttermilk.)

- In a large bowl, combine flour, sugar, baking powder, baking soda, and salt; mix well.

- Whisk eggs, butter, and vanilla into milk mixture, then stir into flour mixture until lumps are gone.

- In a griddle pan or skillet over medium heat, melt 1 teaspoon vegetable shortening. (I prefer to use shortening because it allows the pancakes to cook evenly without burning.) Pour ¼ cup batter into griddle for each pancake and cook for 2 minutes or until bubbles begin to form; turn over and cook for an additional 1 to 2 minutes or until golden brown. Remove to a serving platter and cover with foil to keep warm. Continue in batches until all batter is used.

Easy Glazed Breakfast Pastries

Here's my spin on a pre-packaged toaster strudel that many of you probably have memories of. (I know it used to drive my mom nuts when I ate these kinds of "cookie breakfasts," but hey ... every now and then, you've got to!) Since I've always liked mine frosted, I went ahead and added a glaze to these, but feel free to fill or top with anything you want.

Makes: 12 **Prep Time: 20 min** **Cook Time: 8 min**

1 (14.1-ounce) package rolled refrigerated pie crust

¼ cup chocolate spread

¼ cup seedless raspberry jam

1 cup powdered sugar

1 tablespoon milk

⁘ Preheat oven to 425 degrees F. Coat 2 (13- x 9-inch) Lid-Its or baking sheets with cooking spray. Unroll 1 pie crust and, using a knife, cut into 12 (2- x 3-inch) rectangles, discarding any trimmings.

⁘ Place a teaspoon of chocolate spread on 6 rectangles. Spread evenly leaving a ⅛-inch border. Place a teaspoon of jam in the center of chocolate spread. Top with remaining rectangles. Using a fork, crimp edges to secure and place on a Lid-It. Unroll second pie crust and repeat process.

⁘ Bake for 8 to 10 minutes or until lightly browned. Let cool for 5 minutes, then remove to a wire rack to cool completely.

⁘ In a small bowl, whisk powdered sugar and milk until smooth. Spoon glaze evenly over each pastry. Let glaze harden, then serve.

TARA'S TIP: Not familiar with chocolate spread? No problem. Think of it as a chocolate-like peanut butter which can be found in most supermarkets right next to the regular peanut butter.

All-in-One Smoothie Bowl

Yogurt and granola is my go-to breakfast whenever I'm traveling, especially when I'm going on a plane. Inspired by the delicious contrast of creamy and crunchy, I came up with this thick, spoonable smoothie recipe that features an amazing combination of fruit. My husband, who loves smoothie bowls for breakfast, is crazy about this one!

Serves: 2

½ cup frozen pineapple chunks

½ cup frozen mango chunks

½ cup frozen strawberries

1 banana, cut into chunks

1 cup ice cubes

½ cup regular or almond milk

3 tablespoons honey

¼ cup granola

Assorted fresh fruit for garnish (see Tip)

Prep Time: 10 min

- In a blender, combine pineapple, mango, strawberries, banana, ice, milk, and honey.

- Blend on high until mixture thickens and is smooth, scraping down sides as needed. Pour into 2 cereal bowls.

- Top each bowl with granola and garnish with fresh fruit, as shown. Serve immediately.

TARA'S TIP: For an extra dose of goodness, top each bowl with a dollop of Greek yogurt. As for the fruit, I suggest using your favorites and going with a colorful variety.

OUR GOAL is to
coordinate our colors
with ones that **SUIT**
your lifestyle and
your colorful personality.

Crowd-Pleasing Appetizers

Tex-Mex Party Dip "Cake"

This party starter looks more like a cheesecake than a dip. Plus it brings together everything that I love. It features a crust made with my favorite kind of chips and layer after layer of tasty Tex-Mex toppings. Don't forget to set out a bowl of tortilla chips, as well as some cut-up veggies, so that your guests can dunk away. With a dip like this, you'll really get the party started.

Serves: 10 to 15   Prep Time: 15 min   Cook Time: 12 min   Chill Time: 60 min

1 (9-¾-ounce) package nacho cheese-flavored tortilla chips, finely crushed

¾ stick butter, melted

1 (16-ounce) can refried beans

1 (1-¼-ounce) package taco seasoning mix

1 cup guacamole (see Tip)

1 cup sour cream

1 tomato, seeded and chopped

1 (2-¼-ounce) can sliced black olives, drained

2 cups shredded Monterey Jack cheese

1 fresh jalapeño, thinly sliced (optional)

* Preheat oven to 350 degrees F. Lightly coat a 9-inch springform pan with cooking spray.

* In a medium bowl, combine tortilla chips and butter. Press into bottom and 1-inch up sides of pan. Bake for 12 minutes or until it begins to brown; let cool.

* In a medium bowl, combine refried beans and taco seasoning mix, stirring well. Gently spread over the bottom of the crust, then layer with guacamole and sour cream.

* Garnish top with tomato, olives, cheese, and jalapeño slices, if desired. Cover and chill at least 1 hour before serving. When ready to serve, remove sides of springform pan and serve.

TARA'S TIP: If you've got some extra time and want to make this dip even better, make My Famous Garlicky Guacamole (page 49) and use that instead of store-bought guacamole.

The Ultimate Potato Lover's Dip

I grew up eating potato skins. Back then, we used to hollow out the potatoes and deep fry them. While that was delicious, I wanted to share something a little more creative with you. Here, rather than throwing out the potato pulp that's been scooped out, I've combined it with one of my favorite refrigerated dips to make one heck of a tasty combo. And when you scoop it up with the baked crispy potato skins, it's heavenly.

Serves: 8 to 12   **Prep Time: 15 min**   **Cook Time: 60 min**

6 russet baking potatoes, washed and dried

Cooking spray

1 tablespoon butter, softened

1 (12-ounce) container refrigerated onion dip

½ teaspoon salt

Chopped chives for garnish

∴ Preheat oven to 425 degrees F. Place potatoes on a rimmed 13- x 9-inch Lid-It or baking sheet and completely coat each potato with cooking spray. Bake for 45 minutes or until fork tender. Remove from oven and let cool for 10 to 15 minutes.

∴ Cut potatoes in half lengthwise, and hollow out each half with a spoon, leaving about ¼-inch of the potato pulp on the skin. Place the scooped out pulp in a large microwave-safe bowl and set aside. Cut each potato skin half into 2 or 3 wedges and place back on the Lid-It. Spray wedges with cooking spray.

∴ Add butter, onion dip, and salt to the bowl of potato pulp and beat with an electric mixer until smooth.

∴ When ready to serve, bake the potato skin wedges for 15 to 20 minutes or until crispy. While they're baking, simply reheat the potato dip in the microwave for 1 to 2 minutes or until hot. Sprinkle with chives. Serve the hot dip with the baked potato skins.

Cheddar Bacon Deviled Eggs

I'll admit it – I'm not a huge fan of deviled eggs. However, I think they're a party necessity and I know that a lot of the people close to me really love them. Because of this, I've learned how to make tasty deviled eggs over the years. I load mine up with bacon and cheese, just like I would a baked potato, and I keep my filling a little chunkier to give them more texture.

Makes: 12

Prep Time: 15 min

6 hard-boiled eggs, peeled

¼ cup mayonnaise

2 tablespoons shredded cheddar cheese

1 tablespoon bacon bits, plus some extra for garnish

1 scallion, thinly sliced, with a few pieces reserved for garnish

Cut each egg in half lengthwise; place the yolks in a medium bowl. Place the egg white halves on a paper towel-lined plate.

With a fork, mash the egg yolks. Add mayonnaise, cheese, bacon bits, and scallion; mix well.

With a spoon, pastry bag, or plastic storage bag with the corner snipped (make sure the opening is big enough so the bacon and cheese don't get stuck), fill the egg white halves with the yolk mixture. (The paper towel under the egg whites will prevent them from sliding around while you're filling them.) Garnish with a few bacon bits and scallions. Cover with plastic wrap and refrigerate until ready to serve.

TARA'S TIP: To make perfect, hard-boiled eggs, place 6 eggs in a large saucepan and cover with cold water. Over medium-high heat, bring to a boil. Once boiling, remove from heat, cover, and set a timer for 12 to 15 minutes depending on the size of your eggs. Drain the eggs, rinse with very cold water, and peel.

Extreme Jalapeño Poppers

Jalapeño poppers are a game-day kind of appetizer. When you're watching your favorite team do extreme things, you want an extreme kind of snack at your side. That's why I load my jalapeño poppers with bacon and two kinds of cheeses. Once you've tried our extreme version, it would be hard to go back to ordinary poppers, and why would you want to anyway?

Makes: 2 dozen   Prep Time: 15 min   Cook Time: 20 min   Chill Time: 60 min

1 (8-ounce) package cream cheese, softened

1 cup shredded sharp cheddar cheese

3 tablespoons bacon bits

12 fresh jalapeño peppers, split in half lengthwise, seeds removed

⅓ cup all-purpose flour

2 eggs, lightly beaten

½ cup bread crumbs

Vegetable oil for frying

❖ In a medium bowl, mix together cream cheese, cheddar cheese, and bacon bits until well combined.

❖ Using a spoon, fill each pepper half with the cream cheese mixture. (You may need to use your fingers to really pack it in.) Cover and chill for 1 hour.

❖ Place flour, eggs, and bread crumbs in 3 separate shallow dishes. Dip chilled stuffed pepper halves into the flour, then the eggs, and then the bread crumbs, coating thoroughly. After breading these, keep them refrigerated until you're ready to fry them.

❖ Fill a large deep saucepan or soup pot with 2 inches of oil and heat over medium-high heat until hot, but not smoking. Carefully fry a few peppers at a time, 1 to 3 minutes or until golden. Drain on a paper towel-lined plate and serve immediately.

TARA'S TIP: To add more heat to your jalapeño poppers, just leave some of the seeds in. For me, the hotter the better, so I leave all of the seeds in mine! And remember when working with jalapeños, wear gloves to prevent the oils from burning your skin or eyes.

Pretzel Nuggets with Cheddar Dip

When frozen soft pretzels were first introduced to my family, we were fully on board with it. As kids, instead of having popcorn on movie nights, we asked for pretzels instead. To this day, I get such joy when I make these homemade ones. Plus, when they're paired with my mustardy Cheddar Dip, it's a double bonus!

Makes: 32   **Prep Time: 20 min**   **Cook Time: 20 min**

1 (16.3-ounce) can refrigerated biscuits (8 biscuits)

5 cups water

¼ cup baking soda

1 egg, beaten

Coarse salt for sprinkling

Cheddar Dip

2 tablespoons butter

2 tablespoons all-purpose flour

¾ cup milk

½ teaspoon ground mustard

¼ teaspoon salt

⅛ teaspoon black pepper

2 cups shredded sharp cheddar cheese

❖ Preheat oven to 400 degrees F. Coat 2 rimmed 13- x 9-inch Lid-Its or baking sheets with cooking spray.

❖ On a cutting board, cut each biscuit into quarters, then roll into balls. With a paring knife, cut an "X" about ⅛-inch deep on the top of each dough ball. In a large saucepan, combine water and baking soda. Bring to a boil over medium-high heat, then reduce heat to low. In batches, add dough balls to the simmering water, cooking each batch for about 30 seconds. Remove with a slotted spoon and place on Lid-Its.

❖ Brush each with egg and sprinkle with coarse salt. Bake for 12 to 15 minutes or until golden brown. Let cool for 5 minutes before removing to a serving platter.

❖ Meanwhile, to make the Cheddar Dip, in a medium saucepan over medium heat, melt butter. Whisk in flour and cook for 1 minute or until golden. Slowly whisk in milk, mustard, salt, and pepper and heat until mixture begins to thicken. Stir in cheese and heat until cheese is melted and sauce is smooth. Serve pretzels with cheese sauce.

TARA'S TIP: For an adult version, reduce the amount of milk to ½ cup and add ¼ cup beer to the Cheddar Dip. And if you're wondering what to do with the rest of the bottle of beer, it's the perfect beverage to wash these down with.

Delaware Shore Clams Casino

One of the best parts of living right outside of Philadelphia is that we're not very far from the Delaware shore. So you can bet that I try to spend as much time as possible there once the weather warms up. One of the things that I like to buy when I'm there are the fresh clams. Once I get them home, I stuff them with a delicious mixture and invite a few friends over.

Makes: 36   **Prep Time: 20 min**   **Cook Time: 25 min**

4 slices bacon, finely chopped

1 stick butter

½ cup finely chopped onion

½ cup finely chopped red bell pepper

3 cloves garlic, minced

1 cup plain bread crumbs

1 tablespoon chopped fresh parsley

1 cup dry white wine

2 cups water

36 littleneck clams, rinsed well

❖ Preheat oven to 400 degrees F.

❖ In a large skillet over medium heat, cook bacon 5 to 7 minutes or until crispy, stirring occasionally. Add butter and heat until melted. (Relax. You don't eat like this every day, so enjoy it!) Add onion, bell pepper, and garlic, and cook 3 to 5 minutes or until tender. Remove from heat and stir in bread crumbs and parsley; mix well and set aside.

❖ Meanwhile, in a soup pot over high heat, bring wine and water to a boil. Add clams and cover; steam 5 to 8 minutes or until clams open. Remove clams from pot and discard any which have not opened.

❖ Remove the top shell of each clam and discard. Loosen the clam from the shell, leaving it in the shell. Spoon the bread crumb mixture evenly over the clams, filling each shell. Place on a rimmed 13- x 9-inch Lid-It or baking sheet. Bake for 10 to 12 minutes or until light golden.

TARA'S TIP: I like to serve these on a bed of rock or kosher salt along with some lemon wedges.

Oven-Roasted Buffalo Wing Dings

At almost every get-together or gathering, I check out the buffet to see if they have wings. I'm actually mildly obsessed with them. When I serve them, I like to put out a bunch of different dipping sauces, because I love being able to change the flavor with every dip. And while I think traditional, deep-fried wings are great, baked wings deliver even more flavor. (By the way, in case you were wondering, I prefer "flats" over "drumettes.")

Serves: 6 to 8　　　　**Prep Time: 5 min**　　　　**Cook Time: 60 min**

4 pounds chicken wings, split and thawed, if frozen

1 tablespoon vegetable oil

1 teaspoon salt

½ cup all-purpose flour

1 stick butter

¼ cup cayenne pepper sauce

½ teaspoon garlic powder

- Preheat oven to 425 degrees F. Coat 2 (13- x 9-inch) rimmed Lid-Its or baking sheets with cooking spray.

- In a large bowl, toss wings with oil and salt. Sprinkle wings with flour and toss until evenly coated. Place wings on rimmed Lid-Its. Roast for 30 minutes, then turn wings over and roast for an additional 25 minutes or until crispy.

- Meanwhile, in a small saucepan over medium heat, melt butter. Stir in cayenne pepper sauce and garlic powder.

- Place cooked wings in a large bowl, drizzle with the sauce, and toss until evenly coated. Serve immediately.

TARA'S TIP: Don't get cayenne pepper sauce mixed up with hot pepper sauce. The kind we are using here is much more mild than the stuff that we typically shake on a few drops at a time.

Blue Cheese Dip

If you consider yourself a traditionalist, then you've got to serve your wings with a side of blue cheese. This dip is great with celery, too.

Makes: 2 cups

Prep Time: 5 min

1-½ cups sour cream

¼ cup mayonnaise

1 tablespoon vegetable oil

1 tablespoon white vinegar

4 ounces blue cheese, crumbled

¼ teaspoon salt

¼ teaspoon black pepper

⁘ Place all ingredients in a blender. Blend until well mixed. (If you like a chunkier dip, only add half of the blue cheese to the blender. After it's blended, stir in the remaining crumbles.)

⁘ Serve immediately or cover and chill until ready to use.

Honey Mustard Dip

This dip is creamy, sweet, and tangy. It adds a fun flavor to wings, french fries, and more.

Makes: 2 cups

Prep Time: 5 min

1-¼ cups mayonnaise

⅓ cup honey

⅔ cup vegetable oil

1 tablespoon white vinegar

1 teaspoon minced onion flakes

2 tablespoons chopped fresh parsley

2 tablespoons yellow mustard

⁘ In a medium bowl, whisk together all ingredients until smooth and creamy.

⁘ Serve immediately or cover and chill until ready to use.

Cocktail Meatballs Under Wraps

Whether you're planning a holiday party or you're just having some friends over, make sure you add these to your appetizer spread for a sure-fire hit. They're a cross between traditional pigs-in-a-blanket and sliders. Don't be surprised at how fast these disappear, since they are really novel and tasty!

Makes: 16   **Prep Time: 15 min**   **Cook Time: 12 min**

½ cup ketchup

¼ cup yellow mustard

1 (8-ounce) package refrigerated crescent rolls

½ cup shredded cheddar cheese

16 frozen bite-sized meatballs

1 egg, beaten

1 tablespoon sesame seeds

- In a small bowl, combine ketchup and mustard; mix well and set aside.

- Unroll the dough and separate rolls into 8 triangles. Cut each triangle in half lengthwise, forming 16 triangles. Spread ketchup/mustard sauce evenly over each triangle, and sprinkle evenly with cheese. Place a meatball in the middle of each triangle, then roll up and place seam-side down on a rimmed 13- x 9-inch Lid-It or baking sheet. Brush each with egg then sprinkle evenly with sesame seeds.

- Bake for 12 to 14 minutes or until heated through and golden brown. Serve with remaining sauce.

TARA'S TIP: I love the convenience of store-bought meatballs. If you're a fan from QVC, then you might have even seen me swiping a few of Mama Mancini's meatballs off the table when no one was looking. (No worries, we're friends!) I've fallen in love with how theirs taste just like homemade, and recommend you try this recipe with their meatballs.

Tomato Soup Shooters with Grilled Cheese Dippers

I love doing things that are a bit unexpected, like using things around the house for something you normally wouldn't think to use them for. Shooter glasses are a great way to serve soup as an appetizer. Not only can people help themselves, but they can hold onto their soup and grilled cheese dippers all with one hand. (The other one can help with the dipping!) Besides, who doesn't love tomato soup and grilled cheese?!

Makes: 8   **Prep Time: 10 min**   **Cook Time: 25 min**

1 (14.5-ounce) can diced tomatoes, undrained

1 (8-ounce) can tomato sauce

1 teaspoon sugar

½ teaspoon garlic powder

½ teaspoon salt

¼ teaspoon black pepper

1 cup half-and-half

Grilled Cheese Dippers

4 slices cheddar cheese

4 slices white bread

2 tablespoons butter, softened

4 baby gherkin pickles, cut in half

❖ In a blender, combine tomatoes with their liquid, tomato sauce, sugar, garlic powder, salt, and pepper; blend until smooth. (If you like it a little chunkier, just blend it for less time.) Pour mixture into a large saucepan and bring to a boil over medium-high heat, stirring occasionally.

❖ Reduce heat to low and slowly stir in the half-and-half. Simmer for 8 to 10 minutes or until heated through. (Do not allow to boil.)

❖ Meanwhile to make Grilled Cheese Dippers, place 2 slices of cheese on 1 slice of bread and top with another bread slice, making a cheese sandwich. Repeat with remaining cheese and bread.

❖ Spread butter evenly on both sides of the sandwiches. Cook in a skillet over medium heat until golden on both sides and cheese is melted. Cut crusts off each sandwich and cut each into 4 sticks. Place a toothpick through each pickle half and then through a grilled cheese stick. Pour soup into individual shooter glasses, top each with a grilled cheese stick, and serve immediately.

TARA'S TIP: To keep these warm at a party, fill a 13- x 9-inch baking dish halfway with kosher salt, place it in the oven for a few minutes, and then nestle the filled shooter glasses in the warm salt. Not only is this practical, but it makes the presentation even better!

No-Frills Stuffed Mushrooms

I like to keep my stuffed mushrooms simple. A little sour cream and some butter give these the right amount of richness, while a blend of basic spices and bread crumbs add the perfect flavor and a little crunch. I hope you love what I call my "little pops of heaven" as much as I do!

Makes: 12 to 15　　　**Prep Time: 20 min**　　　**Cook Time: 20 min**

1 pound large
fresh mushrooms

3 tablespoons butter

2 tablespoons sour cream

¼ teaspoon onion powder

¼ teaspoon garlic powder

¼ teaspoon salt

⅛ teaspoon black pepper

¼ cup seasoned
bread crumbs

- Preheat oven to 350 degrees F.

- Gently clean mushrooms by wiping with a damp cloth. (Do not wash them under running water or they'll get mushy.) Remove stems from about three-quarters of the mushrooms; set aside those caps. Finely chop stems and remaining whole mushrooms.

- In a large skillet over medium heat, melt butter; sauté chopped mushrooms for 4 to 5 minutes or until tender. Remove from heat and add all of the remaining ingredients, except bread crumbs. Stir until well combined; mix in bread crumbs.

- Using a teaspoon (the kind you use with your coffee, not the kind you use to measure), stuff mushroom caps with the mixture. Place on an ungreased 13- x 9-inch rimmed Lid-It or baking sheet.

- Bake for 15 to 20 minutes or until heated through. Serve immediately.

TARA'S TIP: If you want to make these a little more gourmet, you can always add some crabmeat, spinach, or shredded cheese to the filling before stuffing them.

Vacation-Worthy Coconut Shrimp

My love affair with coconut shrimp started when I was very young. My family used to go to a fish restaurant where I would always order coconut shrimp as an appetizer. Not only are they delicious, but they're so easy to eat. Now I make these whenever I've got friends and family coming over. I've been told they remind people of being on vacation, which is why I've dubbed them "vacation-worthy."

Serves: 4 to 6　　　**Prep Time: 10 min**　　　**Cook Time: 10 min**

½ cup all-purpose flour

1 tablespoon sugar

½ teaspoon salt

½ teaspoon cayenne pepper (optional)

2 eggs

2 tablespoons water

2-½ cups sweetened shredded coconut

1 pound large shrimp, peeled and deveined, with tails left on

2 cups vegetable oil

- In a shallow dish, combine flour, sugar, salt, and cayenne pepper, if desired; mix well. In a medium bowl, beat together eggs and water. Place coconut in another shallow dish.

- Coat shrimp with flour mixture, then with egg mixture. Roll in coconut, pressing coconut firmly onto shrimp to coat completely.

- In a large deep saucepan or soup pot over medium-high heat, heat oil until hot, but not smoking. Cook shrimp in batches for 1-½ to 2 minutes or until golden and cooked through, turning once during cooking. Drain on a paper towel-lined platter. Serve immediately.

TARA'S TIP: I love dipping these in a sweet sauce! If you do too, then you should try it with my island-style dipping sauce. To make it, in a medium bowl, combine ¾ cup apricot preserves, 2 teaspoons soy sauce, 2 teaspoons honey, and 2 teaspoons Dijon mustard. Whisk it all together until it's well blended. (If you're not going to use it right away, just store it in the fridge.)

Fabulous Fig Jam

Dress up your cheese board or charcuterie platter (that's a fancy way for saying sliced, gourmet meat platter) with this fabulous fig jam. It's super versatile, easy to make, and has such a great flavor. It's wonderful for slathering on rolls and English muffins or smearing on crackers with cheese. I like that it's different than the everyday jams and jellies most people have, which I think makes it just a little more special.

Makes: 1 cup   **Prep Time:** 5 min   **Cook Time:** 35 min   **Chill Time:** 2 hrs

8 ounces dried figs, stems removed, cut in half

1-½ cups water

½ cup sugar

2 tablespoons lemon juice

1 tablespoon honey

In a medium saucepan over medium-high heat, combine all ingredients and bring to a boil. Reduce heat to low and simmer for 35 to 40 minutes or until thickened, stirring occasionally to break down figs.

Place mixture in a jar, cover, and refrigerate for 2 hours or until mixture is chilled.

TARA'S TIP: I've also made bigger batches of this and filled temp-tations ramekins with it, wrapped them up in pretty cellophane, and given these as holiday gifts. My friend MarkCharles asks me for this on every holiday since he loves it so much. I guess I can't blame him.

My Famous Garlicky Guacamole

I bring this dip to almost every single thing I'm asked to come to. People love my guacamole and even if they don't, they tell me that they do, so I just keep bringing it. I recommend serving this with the scoop-style tortilla chips, since they look pretty and make it easy to dig in. This also goes great on Mexican entrees, like tacos, quesadillas, and nachos!

Makes: 1-½ cups

Prep Time: 10 min

3 ripe avocados, halved, pitted, and skin removed

2 tablespoons salsa

4 cloves garlic, minced

¼ teaspoon salt

⅛ teaspoon black pepper

1 tablespoon fresh lime juice (from about ½ a lime)

In a medium bowl, mash avocados with a fork until chunky. Add salsa, garlic, salt, pepper, and lime juice; mix well.

Serve immediately or cover and chill at least 30 minutes or until ready to serve.

TARA'S TIP: Are you ready for an ah-ha moment? If you have any leftover guacamole, make sure to cover it tightly. To do this, press the plastic wrap down onto to the top of the guacamole, pushing out as many air bubbles as possible. This will help to prevent it from turning brown.

Super Simple Sausage Dip

As soon as fall arrives, this becomes my "go-to" dip. It's just got a lot of feel-good flavors going on. This is great for entertaining a crowd or serving when it's just the family coming over. Sometimes I make it just for me! It's simple to make, since you just throw all of the ingredients into your slow cooker, and there's no need to worry about presentation. Just set out the slow cooker and let everyone help themselves!

Serves: 12 to 14   **Prep Time: 5 min**   **Cook Time: 3-½ hrs**

1 pound ground pork sausage (see Tip)

2 (10-ounce) cans diced tomatoes and green chilies

1 (15-ounce) can corn, drained

1 (8-ounce) package cream cheese, cut into chunks

2 cups shredded cheddar cheese

Chopped fresh cilantro for garnish

In a large skillet over medium-high heat, cook sausage for 6 to 8 minutes or until browned, stirring occasionally to break apart; drain liquid.

Place sausage in a 2-½ quart or larger slow cooker. Add tomatoes, corn, cream cheese, and cheddar cheese; mix well. Cover and heat on LOW for 3-½ to 4 hours or on HIGH for 2 hours, or until cheese is melted and mixture is heated through, stirring halfway through. Right before serving, top with chopped cilantro.

TARA'S TIP: Only you know the level of spiciness your family and friends can handle, so make sure you start with sausage that everyone will enjoy. And since it's not polite to dip your fingers into the slow cooker (plus, it will be very hot), don't forget to serve with a side of corn chips.

Sweet & Sour Luau Meatballs

Luaus are so much fun. Besides the grass skirts, coconut bras, and tropical drinks, there's always a lot of unique food being served. It was at a luau on one of my first trips to Hawaii that I discovered how good sweet and sour meatballs could be. Actually, I enjoyed them so much, I came up with my own version of them. These and a few fresh flower leis will add so much excitement to any party!

Serves: 6 to 10   **Prep Time: 10 min**   **Cook Time: 20 min**

1 (10-ounce) jar sweet and sour sauce

¼ cup light brown sugar

¼ cup soy sauce

½ teaspoon ground ginger

1 (35-ounce) package frozen bite-sized meatballs

1-½ cups fresh or frozen mango chunks

1-½ cups fresh or frozen pineapple chunks

¾ cup diced green bell pepper

In a large skillet over medium heat, combine sweet and sour sauce, brown sugar, soy sauce, and ginger; stir until well combined. Add meatballs, reduce heat to medium-low and cover; simmer for 15 to 20 minutes or until heated through.

Stir in the mango, pineapple, and green pepper; cover and simmer for an additional 5 to 7 minutes or until heated through. Serve piping hot.

TARA'S TIP: If you're starting with fresh pineapple, I suggest cutting the pineapple in half lengthwise, carving out each half, and using the pineapple itself as a bowl. It makes for a party-perfect presentation!

Extra-Special Stuffed Artichokes

I love everything about these artichokes. I love the delicate leaves, the savory-buttery filling, and I've always found these to be much more fun to eat than many appetizers or salads. These are perfect for a dinner party since they're a great conversation starter and they'll definitely impress your guests. And the bread crumb stuffing is so good!

Makes: 4   Prep Time: 20 min   Cook Time: 55 min

4 large artichokes

2 tablespoons lemon juice

¾ stick butter

½ cup finely chopped onion

3 cloves garlic, minced

¼ cup white wine

1 cup Italian-flavored bread crumbs

1 tablespoon grated Parmesan cheese

¼ teaspoon black pepper

1 tablespoon olive oil

TARA'S TIP: For even more goodness, serve these with my shortcut Garlic Aioli. To make it, simply place ½ cup of mayo in a blender, along with 1 tablespoon lemon juice, 2 garlic cloves, 1 tablespoon olive oil, and a pinch of black pepper. Blend it all together and you're done!

❁ Trim the bottom of each artichoke so that it sits flat. With a serrated knife, cut about 1 inch off the top of each artichoke. With a pair of kitchen shears, snip the thorny tips off of the upper leaves. Rub cut leaves with lemon juice to prevent them from turning brown.

❁ In a steam basket or large pot over high heat, place artichokes in about 1-inch of water. Bring to a boil, cover, and reduce heat to low. Cook for 25 to 30 minutes or until artichokes are tender. (You'll know they're tender when you can easily pull out a leaf.) Carefully remove artichokes from water (they will be very hot) and drain each one upside down. Place them right side up in a 13- x 9-inch baking dish.

❁ Preheat oven to 375 degrees F.

❁ In a medium skillet over medium heat, melt butter. Add onion and garlic and cook for 5 minutes, stirring occasionally. Add wine and cook for an additional 2 minutes. Remove from heat and stir in bread crumbs, cheese, and pepper. Spread artichoke leaves apart and pack the stuffing between the leaves and over the top, as shown. Drizzle artichokes with olive oil.

❁ Bake for 15 to 20 minutes or until hot. Serve immediately.

WE KNOW THAT THE

smallest

DETAILS MAKE THE

biggest

DIFFERENCE.

THAT'S WHY WE PAY

CLOSE ATTENTION TO

EVERYTHING WE DO.

Simple Soups, Salads, & Sandwiches

Easy Cheesy Macaroni Soup

Trade your fork for a spoon and get ready to dig into this mash-up of two of my favorite comfort foods: soup and macaroni & cheese. Once you experience this, it's hard not to think about it all the time. As you can imagine, it's really popular with kids too. Good thing it's so easy to make, because I think this one's going to be a regular on your weekday dinner menu!

Serves: 4 to 6   **Prep Time: 10 min**   **Cook Time: 15 min**

1 cup elbow macaroni

½ stick butter

⅓ cup all-purpose flour

2 cups chicken or vegetable broth

1 cup whole milk

1 (8-ounce) block cheddar cheese, shredded (see Tip)

½ cup cooked diced ham

- Cook elbow macaroni according to package instructions. Drain and rinse.

- Meanwhile, in a soup pot over medium heat, melt butter. Whisk in flour and cook for 1 minute or until mixture is golden. Slowly whisk in the broth and milk; bring to a boil and cook until thickened, stirring occasionally.

- Reduce heat to low and stir in cheese; simmer until melted. Add ham and cooked macaroni and cook for an additional 5 minutes or until heated through. Serve and enjoy.

TARA'S TIP: I prefer shredding a block of cheese, rather than starting with pre-shredded cheese. I just find that the block of cheese melts smoother. However, if you're looking to save some additional time or want to use shredded cheese you've already got in the refrigerator, you'll need about 2 cups.

Old World Chicken Soup

This here's the real McCoy ... a soup just like the one grandma used to make. I didn't take any shortcuts because I think everyone should have at least one from-scratch chicken soup in their recipe collection. This one is going to deliver all that feel-good comfort you crave, along with lots of heartiness to keep you full and satisfied.

Serves: 8 to 10　　　**Prep Time: 15 min**　　　**Cook Time: 1-¼ hrs**

2 tablespoons vegetable oil

1 onion, cut into 1-inch chunks

3 carrots, cut into 1-inch chunks

2 celery stalks, cut into 1-inch chunks

1 (3-pound) chicken, cut into 8 pieces

12 cups cold water

2 tablespoons chicken base (See Tip)

1 teaspoon dried thyme

1 teaspoon salt

½ teaspoon black pepper

8 ounces bowtie noodles, cooked according to package directions

1 tablespoon chopped fresh parsley

In a soup pot over medium-high heat, heat oil until hot; sauté onion, carrots, and celery for 5 to 7 minutes or until vegetables begin to brown. Add chicken, water, chicken base, thyme, salt, and pepper, and bring to a boil. Reduce heat to low and simmer for 1 hour or until chicken falls off the bones easily.

Using tongs, remove chicken from soup; allow chicken to cool slightly. Remove the bones and skin and discard them. Then, cut the chicken into bite-sized pieces and return to soup. Stir in bowtie noodles and parsley, and simmer for an additional 5 minutes or until heated through. Now all you have to do is grab a ladle and dish up bowls of comfort.

TARA'S TIP: For a really rich-tasting chicken broth, you need to add chicken base. If you've never used it before, it's basically a paste that turns "blah" soup into "best-ever" soup. You can find it sold in jars or tubs at the grocery store, near the canned soup broths.

Slow Cooker Taco Soup

This is basically just another great way for me to enjoy some of my favorite Mexican flavors. The idea for this came to me while I was enjoying a heaping plate of nachos. I thought, why can't I just leave out the chips and make this into a soup? Also, why not make it in my slow cooker so that by the time I get home the whole house smells like taco paradise?

Serves: 6 to 8   Prep Time: 10 min   Cook Time: 7 hrs

1 tablespoon vegetable oil

1 pound ground beef

1 onion, chopped

2 tablespoons water

1 (1.25-ounce) package taco seasoning

1 (15-ounce) can black beans, rinsed and drained

1 (16-ounce) can chili beans, undrained

2 cups frozen corn

2 cups beef broth

1 (8-ounce) can tomato sauce

1 (10-ounce) can diced tomatoes with chilies, undrained

- In a large skillet over medium-high heat, heat oil until hot; cook ground beef and onion until no pink remains in the beef, stirring to crumble beef as it cooks. Drain excess liquid. Stir in water and taco seasoning.

- In a 5-quart or larger slow cooker, add both beans, corn, broth, tomato sauce, and diced tomatoes. Spoon cooked ground beef over top.

- Cover and cook on LOW 7 hours or on HIGH 3 hours or until bubbling hot.

TARA'S TIP: When the soup is just about done, set out a few of your favorite taco toppings. Then when it's ready to serve, everyone can finish their own bowl however they like. To get you started, I suggest shredded cheese, sour cream, and tortilla chips.

Philly Cheesesteak Bread Bowl Soup

If it were up to me, I would turn everything into a soup. (Okay, maybe not everything, but lots of things.) Living in Philly, I've had cheesesteak once or twice (or a dozen) times in my life, so, once I figured out how to make mac & cheese as a soup (page 56) I figured it was time to try it with another yummy classic. As you can guess, it was a success!

Serves: 3 to 4   **Prep Time: 15 min**   **Cook Time: 12 min**

4 large kaiser rolls

1 tablespoon vegetable oil

1 onion, cut in half and thinly sliced

½ green bell pepper, diced

4 cups beef broth

½ teaspoon garlic powder

½ teaspoon salt

¼ teaspoon black pepper

½ cup water

3 tablespoons all-purpose flour

½ pound deli roast beef, cut into ½-inch strips

¼ cup cheese sauce, warmed (I used Cheez Whiz®)

- Cut a 2- to 3-inch circle off the top of each roll and remove. Hollow out rolls, leaving 1-inch of bread around sides to make a bowl. (Yes, you're going to serve the soup out of a bread bowl.)

- In a large skillet over medium-high heat, heat oil until hot. Sauté onion and bell pepper for 5 to 7 minutes or until softened. Add broth, garlic powder, salt, and pepper; bring to a boil.

- Meanwhile, in a small bowl, whisk water and flour until smooth. Slowly whisk into broth mixture and simmer until thickened. Stir in roast beef and heat for 1 to 2 minutes or until heated through.

- Spoon soup into bread bowls and drizzle with cheese sauce. Serve immediately.

TARA'S TIP: If you prefer to serve this in a traditional soup bowl, go ahead. If you do, I recommend topping each bowl with a handful of homemade croutons. After all, what's a Philly cheesesteak without the bread?

Tortellini Vegetable Soup

Honestly, I don't think people make enough vegetable soups. I don't understand why—they're so delicious! Maybe they're worried about having to chop and dice all the veggies. If that's the case, they should just start with frozen ones, like I do! Frozen veggies are fresh and convenient. Here, I combine them with frozen tortellini for a hearty soup that tastes like you worked on it all day long.

Makes: 6 to 8 cups **Prep Time: 10 min** **Cook Time: 20 min**

1 tablespoon olive oil, plus extra for drizzling

½ cup chopped onion

1 stalk celery, thinly sliced

3 cloves garlic, minced

8 cups vegetable broth

5 tablespoons tomato paste

2 cups frozen mixed vegetables

1 teaspoon salt

½ teaspoon black pepper

2-½ cups frozen cheese tortellini

In a soup pot over medium heat, heat 1 tablespoon oil until hot. Add onion, celery, and garlic and cook for about 5 minutes, stirring occasionally, until the veggies are tender. Add broth, tomato paste, mixed vegetables, salt, and pepper; give it a stir and bring to a boil. Reduce heat to low and simmer for 10 minutes.

Add tortellini and cook for 5 minutes or until pasta is tender. Serve immediately with a drizzle of olive oil over each bowl.

TARA'S TIP: Pasta has a tendency to soak up the broth in soup, so if you let it sit for too long, you might find you'll need to add a bit more broth. If that's the case, simply add more until it's the consistency you like.

Broccoli & Brie Bistro Soup

My husband, Ed, loves anything with brie. I love anything with broccoli. We both are big fans of soup. So, I had the idea of bringing all of our loves together and coming up with this amazing bistro-style soup that's so good, you'll want to lick the bowl when you're done. The first time I made it, Ed and I were so busy slurping up spoonful after spoonful that we barely said a word to each other during dinner!

Serves: 4 to 6   **Prep Time: 10 min**   **Cook Time: 25 min**

4 cups chicken broth

4 cups coarsely chopped broccoli

½ cup chopped onion

½ teaspoon salt

½ teaspoon black pepper

½ stick butter

6 tablespoons all-purpose flour

1-½ cups half-and-half

1 (8-ounce) package Brie cheese, rind removed and cut into 1-inch chunks

- In a soup pot over high heat, combine broth, broccoli, onion, salt, and pepper; bring to a boil. Reduce heat to low and simmer for 10 to 12 minutes or until broccoli is tender.

- Meanwhile, in a skillet over medium heat, melt butter; whisk in flour. Cook for about 1 minute or until golden.

- Slowly, whisk the flour mixture into the soup, stirring until thickened; simmer for 5 minutes. Slowly stir in half-and-half, mixing well. Add cheese, stir, and heat until cheese is melted. Ladle it into bowls and bon appetite!

TARA'S TIP: When it's just the two of us having this for dinner, I serve this with a loaf of crusty French bread for dunking. But when I'm making this for company, I top each bowl with a small wedge of brie. It adds that extra wow factor. If you'd like more "wow," then make sure you pick up an extra package of Brie while you're at the grocery store.

Bacon-Dressed Spinach Salad

Nine times out of ten, I make my own dressing for my salads. That's not to say I never use bottled dressings, but there's something about making them homemade that makes salads a little more special. This salad, which is a favorite of mine, is topped with a warm bacon dressing that I came up with after trying to make it many, many times. Finally I discovered the perfect combo of ingredients. Now I can make this in my sleep.

Serves: 3 to 4   **Prep Time: 10 min**   **Cook Time: 8 min**

Hot Bacon Dressing

8 slices bacon, chopped

¼ cup apple cider vinegar

2 teaspoons lemon juice

2 tablespoons sugar

¼ teaspoon black pepper

1 (10-ounce) package
fresh spinach

1 hard-boiled egg, chopped

1 tablespoon chopped
red onion

1 green apple, sliced
into wedges

To make the Hot Bacon Dressing, in a large skillet over medium-high heat, cook bacon until crisp, leaving the bacon and drippings in the pan. Add vinegar, lemon juice, sugar, and pepper; mix well and heat for about 2 minutes or until the sugar is dissolved.

In a large bowl, place the spinach; add dressing and toss to coat. Top with egg, onion, and sliced apples. Serve immediately.

TARA'S TIP: On days when I know I'm going to be home late from QVC, I'll get everything prepped before I go. That way, when I get home, I just have to heat the dressing and within minutes, dinner is served. On those nights, I often top the salad with some cooked chicken or shrimp to make it a complete meal.

Israeli-Style Spoon Salad

When my husband, Ed, and I went to Israel, we got to sample so many different delicious foods. One of them was an Israeli salad, which is a chopped salad that has tomatoes, cucumbers, onion, and more. Not only did it taste great, but I loved how small everything was chopped—you could eat it with a spoon! When I got back home, I made my own version and it's been a regular part of our summertime salad routine.

Serves: 6 to 8   **Prep Time: 15 min**   **Chill Time: 2 hrs**

3 tomatoes, seeded and diced

2 green bell peppers, seeded and diced

2 cucumbers, peeled, seeded, and diced

4 radishes, diced

¼ cup chopped onion

1 (15.5-ounce) can chick peas, rinsed and drained

1 (2-¼ ounce) can sliced black olives, drained

Lemon Vinaigrette

⅓ cup olive oil

4 teaspoons white vinegar

3 tablespoons lemon juice

1-½ teaspoons salt

½ teaspoon black pepper

⁘ In a large bowl, combine tomatoes, bell peppers, cucumbers, radishes, onion, chick peas, and olives.

⁘ To make the Lemon Vinaigrette, in a small bowl, combine the remaining ingredients; mix well. Pour the dressing over the vegetables and toss until they're well coated.

⁘ Cover and chill for at least 2 hours or overnight, allowing the mixture to marinate before serving.

TARA'S TIP: This is such a pretty salad to make for parties. When I do, I often serve it on ceramic Asian-style soup spoons. It makes for such a great presentation!

Grilled Romaine with Balsamic Glaze

It's time to get a little fancy with your salads, and you don't have to wait for company to do it! All right, this may not be your everyday dinner salad, but when the weather's nice and you're thinking about firing up the grill anyway ... why not? From the syrupy drizzle of Balsamic Glaze to the subtly sweet crunch of pine nuts, this salad is going to rock your taste buds.

Serves: 4   Prep Time: 10 min   Cook Time: 25 min

Balsamic Glaze

1 cup balsamic vinegar

½ cup light brown sugar

2 (¼-inch-thick) slices red onion

1 tablespoon olive oil

1 large head romaine lettuce, cut in half lengthwise with core intact

½ cup cherry tomatoes, cut in half

¼ cup crumbled goat cheese

1 tablespoon pine nuts

❖ Preheat grill to medium heat.

❖ To make Balsamic Glaze, in a medium saucepan over high heat, bring balsamic vinegar to a boil. Stir in brown sugar, reduce heat to low, and simmer for 15 to 18 minutes or until mixture thickens slightly. Remove from heat.

❖ Place sliced onions on the grill and cook for 4 to 5 minutes per side or until they begin to caramelize. (The onions will separate as they cook; that's no problem.) Drizzle olive oil on cut sides of romaine and place on grill, cut-side down. Cook for 4 to 5 minutes per side or just until the edges of the lettuce begin to brown. (And for those of you who aren't into grilling, you can make this on a grill pan, no worries.)

❖ Place romaine on a platter; cut-side up. Top each half with grilled onions, tomatoes, goat cheese, pine nuts, and a drizzle of balsamic glaze. Cut each half in half and enjoy.

TARA'S TIP: There's a pretty good chance you're going to end up with some leftover Balsamic Glaze. Not to worry, you can store it! Just put it in a microwave-safe container and keep it in the refrigerator. When you want to use it again, all you have to do is microwave it for a few seconds until it's pourable.

Shanghai Cabbage Salad

I find that people who get bored of eating salads are people who make the same salads over and over again. The trick to being a salad lover is to add variety. There are so many different ways to mix it up, there's really no need to get stuck with boring iceberg and ranch dressing every time. This cabbage salad features an Asian flair that's really yummy. Sometimes I add chicken or shrimp and make it a main dish.

Serves: 4 to 6　　　**Prep Time: 15 min**　　　**Cook Time: 5 min**

Warm Asian Dressing

2 tablespoons sesame oil

⅓ cup sesame seeds

4 cloves garlic, minced

¼ cup soy sauce

¼ cup white vinegar

½ cup sugar

½ cup vegetable oil

1 head Napa or Chinese cabbage, shredded

1 carrot, peeled and shredded

½ pound snow peas, trimmed

½ red bell pepper, slivered

To make the Warm Asian Dressing, in a large skillet over medium heat, heat sesame oil until hot; sauté sesame seeds and garlic for 3 to 5 minutes or until seeds are golden. Add soy sauce, vinegar, sugar, and vegetable oil. Cook for 1 minute or until sugar is dissolved; set aside.

In a large bowl, combine cabbage, carrot, snow peas, and bell pepper. Add dressing and toss until evenly coated. Serve immediately.

TARA'S TIP: In the summer, I like to add in a can of drained mandarin oranges or lychee nuts. It makes this salad even more refreshing!

Cowboy Stacked Salad

I hope you didn't think this was going to be a lighter salad, because this one is anything but. This Texas-sized salad is meant to feed a cowboy's hearty appetite, which makes it great for parties or big family dinners. It's absolutely decadent, with layer upon layer of deliciousness. I just love watching everyone take their first bite—who knew I could get so many people to love a salad?!

Serves: 6 to 8

Prep Time: 15 min

Creamy Ranch Dressing

1 cup mayonnaise

1 cup sour cream

1 (1-ounce) package dry ranch-style dressing mix

6 corn muffins

2 (16-ounce) cans kidney beans, rinsed and drained

1 green bell pepper, chopped

1 (16-ounce) package frozen corn, thawed

3 large tomatoes, chopped

10 slices bacon, cooked and crumbled

2 cups shredded Mexican cheese blend

6 scallions, sliced

To make the Creamy Ranch Dressing, in a small bowl, combine the mayonnaise, sour cream, and dressing mix; set aside.

Crumble half of the corn muffins into a large bowl or trifle dish. Place a layer of beans over corn muffins, then continue layering with bell pepper, half of the dressing mixture, corn, tomatoes, bacon, remaining corn muffins, the rest of the dressing, and cheese. Top with scallions.

Serve immediately or cover and chill until ready to use.

TARA'S TIP: This looks great in a 3-quart or larger Old World Confetti bowl!

Colorful Confetti Salad

Colorful salads like this one aren't just pretty to look at, they're full of flavors and nutrition too. In this one, I've included an incredible mix of protein-packed ingredients like edamame and black beans, as well as vitamin-rich ones like tomatoes and peppers. My favorite thing about this salad is how well the Red Wine Vinaigrette brings all the veggies together. I especially love how it brings out the mild, sweet flavor of the red onion.

Serves: 6 to 8　　　**Prep Time: 20 min**　　　**Chill Time: 30 min**

2 cups shelled edamame, cooked according to package directions

1 (15-ounce) can black beans, rinsed and drained

1 cup frozen corn, thawed and drained

1 red bell pepper, chopped

2 ripe plum tomatoes, cut into ½-inch chunks

½ cup chopped red onion

2 tablespoons chopped fresh cilantro

Red Wine Vinaigrette

½ cup olive oil

⅓ cup red wine vinegar

1 tablespoon lemon juice

3 cloves garlic, minced

1 teaspoon salt

½ teaspoon black pepper

In a large bowl, combine all the ingredients, except the ones used to make the Red Wine Vinaigrette. Toss until well combined.

To make the Red Wine Vinaigrette, in a small bowl, combine the olive oil, vinegar, lemon juice, garlic, salt, and pepper; whisk until thoroughly combined. Pour over salad and toss until evenly coated. Refrigerate for at least 30 minutes or until ready to serve.

TARA'S TIP: If you want to serve this as a main dish or just want to hearty it up even more, add some chicken or shrimp.

Cranberry Citrus Quinoa Salad

Quinoa doesn't always have to be served hot! Here it's the star of a fresh-tasting salad. I love how the citrusy dressing complements the fresh broccoli, while the walnuts add a nice crunch to every bite. (I'm always adding something crunchy to my salads!) If you weren't a big fan of quinoa before, give this a try, and I'm pretty confident that it will change your mind!

Serves: 4 to 6

Prep Time: 15 min

Citrus Dressing

¼ cup vegetable oil

3 tablespoons rice wine vinegar

Juice of ½ an orange

¾ teaspoon salt

¼ teaspoon black pepper

1 cup dry quinoa, cooked according to package directions and cooled

½ an orange, peeled and cut into 1-inch pieces

2 cups fresh broccoli florets, blanched

¾ cup dried cranberries

1 cup coarsely chopped toasted walnuts

¼ cup chopped red onion

⁖ To make the Citrus Dressing, in a small bowl, whisk oil, vinegar, orange juice, salt, and pepper until it emulsifies (comes together); set aside.

⁖ In a large bowl, combine quinoa, orange pieces, broccoli, cranberries, walnuts, and onion. Pour dressing over salad and toss until evenly coated. Serve or refrigerate until ready to serve.

> TARA'S TIP: If you don't want to trim and cut the broccoli into florets, you can just thaw and drain a bag of frozen broccoli florets. I love time savers!

Deserted Island BLT Sandwiches

If I were on a deserted island, this is the sandwich that I would ask to be left with. It's a sandwich that pulls at my heartstrings, because my mom would make a classic version of it all the time when I was growing up. When I got older and started experimenting with different flavors, I found that I could add avocado and garlicky mayo to make it even better. Now everything I love is in this sandwich.

Makes: 4 **Prep Time: 10 min** **Cook Time: 15 min**

8 slices thick-cut bacon

Coarse black pepper for sprinkling

2 tablespoons brown sugar

1 ripe avocado, pitted and peeled

⅓ cup mayonnaise

3 cloves garlic, minced

8 slices sourdough bread

16 leaves Boston Bibb lettuce

8 slices tomato

Preheat oven to 425 degrees F. Place bacon on a rimmed Lid-It or baking sheet. Sprinkle bacon evenly with pepper and brown sugar. Bake for 15 to 18 minutes or until crispy. Remove to a wire rack to cool.

In a small bowl, mash avocado; stir in mayonnaise and garlic. Meanwhile, toast the bread. Spread avocado mixture evenly on the toasted bread.

Top 4 slices of bread with lettuce, tomato, and the caramelized bacon. Top with remaining bread. Cut sandwiches in half and serve immediately.

TARA'S TIP: If you only need to make one or two sandwiches, I suggest cooking all of the bacon and keeping the rest of it in the fridge or freezer for when you're ready for the rest of your sandwiches. The bacon reheats well in the microwave—it just takes a few seconds.

The Real Deal Veggie Burgers

I have quite a few friends and loved ones who prefer to eat lighter, so whenever I'm entertaining, I make both beef burgers and veggie burgers. Unlike some veggie burgers that look like hockey pucks, these are full of flavors and textures that people really love. I like to say they've got a lot of "oomph" to them. They're so hearty, no one ever feels like they're missing out—and that's how you know they're the real deal!

Makes: 4　　　**Prep Time: 15 min**　　　**Cook Time: 10 min**

1 (15-ounce) can black beans, rinsed and drained, divided

2 cups (6 ounces) chopped mushrooms

1 cup chopped fresh broccoli florets

¾ cup frozen corn, thawed

¼ cup minced onion

1 teaspoon garlic powder

1 teaspoon salt

¼ teaspoon black pepper

2 eggs, beaten

1 tablespoon steak sauce

1 cup bread crumbs

¼ cup grated Parmesan cheese

1 tablespoon olive oil

4 whole wheat rolls

⁜ In a medium bowl, mash 1 cup black beans. Place the rest of the beans in a large bowl along with the mushrooms, broccoli, corn, onion, garlic powder, salt, and pepper; mix well. Add the mashed black beans, eggs, steak sauce, bread crumbs, and Parmesan cheese; mix just until combined. Form mixture into 4 patties.

⁜ In a large skillet over medium-high heat, heat oil until hot; cook burgers for 4 to 5 minutes per side, or until burgers firm up and are heated through. Place each burger on a roll and serve.

Artichoke & Chicken Melty Panini

This amazing, melty, mouthwatering panini was inspired by one of my favorite dips. No, really—at home I'm always using dips as spreads on sandwiches. It's such an easy way to make a sandwich taste really good. The garlicky-cheese spread that I use here, paired with spinach, chicken, red peppers, and my favorite, artichokes, makes for a perfect panini.

Makes: 4   Prep Time: 10 min   Cook Time: 20 min

1 (8-ounce) package cream cheese, softened

1-½ cups shredded mozzarella cheese

¼ cup grated Parmesan cheese

1 teaspoon garlic powder

4 ciabatta rolls, cut in half

1 cup baby spinach

1 cup frozen grilled chicken strips, thawed

½ cup roasted red pepper strips, drained

1 (12-ounce) jar marinated artichoke hearts, drained and coarsely chopped

1 tablespoon olive oil

- In a medium bowl, combine cream cheese, mozzarella cheese, Parmesan cheese, and garlic powder; mix well. Spread mixture over the cut side of bottom and top of each roll.

- On bottom halves of rolls, layer spinach, chicken, peppers, and artichokes. Cover with tops of rolls.

- Heat a panini press to medium-high heat. Brush both sides of panini press with oil. Grill sandwiches in batches for 4 to 5 minutes or until golden and heated through. Repeat with remaining sandwiches, cut in half, and serve.

Deli-Style Reuben Sliders

Come on, I grew up in New York—you know I had to include some kind of New York deli classic in here! As a lover of anything with Russian dressing on it, I chose to recreate the traditional Reuben. These sliders are perfect for parties or get-togethers because they're the perfect size and they're easy to grab and go.

Makes: 12　　　**Prep Time: 10 min**　　　**Cook Time: 15 min**

1 (12-ounce) package (12) attached dinner rolls (see Tip)

½ cup Russian dressing

1 pound thinly sliced deli corned beef

1 (16-ounce) package sauerkraut, drained well

6 slices Swiss cheese

2 tablespoons butter, melted

1 teaspoon caraway seeds

- Preheat oven to 350 degrees F.

- Slice rolls in half all at once and place bottom half on a 13- x 9-inch Lid-It or baking sheet. Spread dressing on cut sides of rolls. Layer bottom half evenly with corned beef, sauerkraut, and Swiss cheese. Place top of rolls on Swiss cheese.

- Brush top of rolls with butter, then sprinkle with caraway seeds. Cover with aluminum foil.

- Bake for 18 to 20 minutes or until the meat is heated through and the cheese is melted. Slice between the rolls to make into individual sliders.

TARA'S TIP: To make this extra-easy, I make this as one big sandwich. That means I don't separate or cut the individual rolls until it's baked and ready to serve.

Summer Caprese Grilled Cheese

Every summer, the thing I look forward to the most is making a fresh caprese salad using tomatoes and herbs from my own garden. (I grow a number of different herbs each year, but basil is an absolute must-have.) Sometimes, instead of a salad, I just make this amazing caprese sandwich. I'm just a couple of cows and a wheat farm away from having a truly homegrown meal.

Makes: 4   **Prep Time: 5 min**   **Cook Time: 15 min**

½ cup garlic and herb cheese spread

8 slices Italian bread

3 plum tomatoes, sliced ¼-inch thick

1 (8-ounce) ball fresh mozzarella cheese, sliced

½ cup fresh basil leaves

Coarse black pepper for sprinkling

¼ cup olive oil

- Preheat oven to 325 degrees F.

- Evenly spread the cheese spread on each slice of bread. Layer 4 slices of bread with tomato, mozzarella cheese, basil leaves, and a sprinkle of pepper. Place remaining bread slices on top and brush both sides of sandwiches with olive oil.

- In a skillet or griddle pan over medium-low heat, cook sandwiches in batches until golden brown on both sides. Transfer to a Lid-It or baking sheet and place in oven for 10 to 15 minutes or until cheese begins to melt. With a serrated knife, cut each sandwich in half and serve immediately.

TARA'S TIP: The key to making this just perfect, is to let the cheese melt slightly, but not to the point that it totally oozes out of the sandwich. (Check out the photo to see what I mean!)

Our artisans have been
hand painting
ceramics for years,
and each has his or her
own style — which makes
every piece a
one-of-a-kind
collectable.

Prize-Worthy Poultry

Not-Your-Grandma's Chicken Pot Pie

I love a classic, grandma-style chicken pot pie, but a lot of times it's just too labor intensive to make, even if you're starting with store-bought shortcuts. This version is more like a casserole-style, which means it's much easier to make. You still get all of the flavors you expect, but you don't have to fuss as much!

Serves: 4 to 6　　**Prep Time: 15 min**　　**Cook Time: 40 min**

1 stick butter, divided

1 cup thinly sliced carrots

½ cup thinly sliced celery

1 cup sliced mushrooms

¾ cup frozen green peas

⅓ cup all-purpose flour

1-¾ cups chicken broth

¾ cup milk

2-½ cups diced cooked chicken

½ teaspoon onion powder

¾ teaspoon salt

¼ teaspoon black pepper

1 (6-ounce) package stuffing mix, prepared according to package directions

❖ Preheat oven to 375 degrees F.

❖ In a deep skillet over medium heat, melt ½ stick butter; cook the carrots and celery for 4 to 5 minutes or until tender. Add mushrooms and peas and continue to cook for 3 minutes, stirring occasionally. Remove vegetables to a bowl; set aside.

❖ Melt remaining ½ stick butter in same skillet, whisk in the flour, and cook for 1 minute or until golden, stirring constantly. Slowly whisk in chicken broth and milk and cook until thickened, stirring occasionally. Remove from heat and stir in chicken, onion powder, salt, pepper, and the reserved vegetables that you set aside.

❖ Pour chicken filling into a pie dish. With your fingers, crumble prepared stuffing evenly over top. Place pie dish on a rimmed 13- x 9-inch Lid-It or baking sheet (it might bubble over when it bakes!). Bake for 25 to 30 minutes or until stuffing crust is golden and filling is bubbly hot. Then serve and enjoy.

TARA'S TIP: You can start with a rotisserie chicken (my favorite shortcut!), leftover grilled or roasted chicken from last night's dinner, or cooked chicken from the freezer aisle of your supermarket. You can even make this using cooked turkey, if you prefer.

One-Pan
BBQ Chicken Feast

When you've had a long day but still need to put dinner on the table, nothing beats a throw-it-all-together one-pan meal. To make this a little more homemade, I doctor up a bottle of my favorite barbecue sauce with some honey and bacon bits. It's simple, it's filling, and everyone loves it.

Serves: 4 to 5   **Prep Time: 10 min**   **Cook Time: 65 min**

1 (3-½ to 4-pound) chicken, cut into 8 pieces

Salt for sprinkling

Black pepper for sprinkling

1 cup barbecue sauce

½ cup honey

3 tablespoons bacon bits

4 ears frozen mini corn on the cob, thawed (see Tip)

Preheat oven to 350 degrees F. Sprinkle chicken evenly with salt and pepper and place on a rimmed 13- x 9-inch Lid-It or baking sheet. Roast for 35 minutes, then remove from oven.

Meanwhile, in a small bowl, combine barbecue sauce, honey, and bacon bits; mix well. Brush half the sauce mixture evenly on both sides of chicken. Return to oven and roast for an additional 15 minutes.

Brush remaining barbecue sauce mixture on chicken. Cut the corn on the cob into 1-inch slices and place around the chicken. Return to oven and continue to roast for about 15 more minutes or until chicken is no longer pink in center.

TARA'S TIP: When fresh corn is in season, you can bet that I use it rather than frozen corn on the cob.

Anytime Buttermilk Fried Chicken

Whenever I think of fried chicken, I think of Jones Beach in New York. Mom always used to make fried chicken for us to take and eat on the sand. Actually, we would eat it on Dad's old green army blanket (I can still remember how itchy it was!). We would eat it cold, and no one complained. It was so good, we would eat it any time, any way. This holds true for my version of fried chicken—eat it however and whenever you like!

Serves: 4 to 5   **Prep Time: 35 min**   **Cook Time: 50 min**

1 (3- to 3-½-pound) chicken, cut into 8 pieces

2 cups biscuit baking mix

2 teaspoons paprika

1 teaspoon garlic powder

1 tablespoon salt

2 teaspoons black pepper

1 cup buttermilk

2 tablespoons hot sauce

2 cups vegetable oil

- Place chicken in a large bowl of ice water; let sit 30 minutes.

- In a second large bowl, combine baking mix, paprika, garlic powder, salt, and pepper; mix well. In another large bowl, mix buttermilk and hot sauce.

- Remove chicken from water and pat dry with paper towels. Dip chicken in seasoned baking mix, then in buttermilk mixture, and then back in the seasoned baking mix, coating completely each time.

- In a large deep skillet over medium-low heat, heat oil until hot, but not smoking. Fry chicken in batches, for 10 to 12 minutes per side or until golden and no longer pink in center. (The breasts may take longer.) Drain on a wire rack over a Lid-It or baking sheet. Serve immediately.

TARA'S TIP: If you want to reheat cold chicken, just stick it in a 300 degree oven for about 20 minutes.

Gail's Favorite Chicken Cacciatore

My mom, Gail, loves chicken cacciatore. We actually had it quite often growing up because it was so easy to make. Even though I'm not a huge fan of red sauce, I always liked her chicken cacciatore because of the chunks of tomato she'd add in. So you don't miss any of the sauce, make sure you serve this over pasta, rice, or with a side of crusty, Italian bread.

Serves: 4 to 5   **Prep Time: 15 min**   **Cook Time: 50 min**

⅓ cup olive oil

2 bell peppers (1 red and 1 green), cut into strips

½ pound mushrooms, quartered

1 large onion, cut in half, then cut into thin slices

3 cloves garlic, minced

½ cup all-purpose flour

½ teaspoon salt

¼ teaspoon black pepper

1 (3- to 3-½-pound) chicken, cut into 8 pieces

1 (24-ounce) jar spaghetti sauce

2 plum tomatoes, chopped

¼ cup water

¼ cup dry red wine (optional)

❖ In a soup pot over medium-high heat, heat oil until hot. Add bell peppers, mushrooms, onion, and garlic, and sauté for 5 minutes or until tender. Remove to a bowl, leaving any pan drippings in the pot.

❖ Meanwhile, combine flour, salt, and pepper in a shallow dish. Dip chicken into flour mixture, one piece at a time, coating completely. In the same soup pot, cook chicken pieces for 6 to 8 minutes per side or until browned.

❖ Return cooked vegetables to the pot and add spaghetti sauce, tomatoes, water, and the red wine, if desired; mix well. Reduce heat to medium-low and simmer for 30 to 40 minutes or until chicken is tender and no longer pink in center. Serve chicken topped with sauce.

Greek-Style Chicken & Potatoes

My husband, Ed, and I ate a dish like this twice while we were in the beautiful Greek isle of Santorini. I loved how fresh-tasting their food was, so when I got home I came up with my own chicken feast that mirrors their flavors and traditions. This is a hearty meal with a welcome Mediterranean taste that's probably a little different from what you normally serve for dinner, but I bet you're going to love it as much as we do.

Serves: 4 to 5   **Prep Time: 5 min**   **Cook Time: 55 min**

1 (32-ounce) package frozen seasoned potato wedges, thawed

½ cup olive oil

¼ cup lemon juice

3 tablespoons fresh oregano, chopped, plus extra for sprinkling

1 teaspoon salt

½ teaspoon black pepper

1 teaspoon garlic powder

2-½ to 3 pounds bone-in, skin-on, chicken thighs

1 lemon, cut into wedges

1 cup grape tomatoes, cut in half

½ cup pitted Kalamata olives

1 cup crumbled feta cheese

- Preheat oven to 350 degrees F. Place potato wedges in a large bowl.

- In another large bowl, combine oil, lemon juice, 3 tablespoons oregano, the salt, pepper, and garlic powder; mix well. (If you don't have fresh oregano, use 2 teaspoons of dried instead.) Pour half of the seasoned oil mixture over the potato wedges and toss. Transfer to a 3.5-quart casserole dish or 13- x 9-inch baking dish and bake for 10 minutes.

- Meanwhile, toss the chicken with the remaining seasoned oil until evenly coated. In a large skillet over medium-high heat, sauté chicken for 5 minutes per side or until both sides are browned. Place chicken over potatoes, skin-side up, and arrange lemon wedges around chicken.

- Roast for 45 to 50 minutes or until no pink remains in chicken and the potatoes are hot. Sprinkle with tomatoes, olives, cheese, and extra oregano. Serve immediately.

TARA'S TIP: Want to make dinner really fun? Ask Google or Siri to play the soundtrack from "My Big Fat Greek Wedding." Breaking dishes (especially temp-tations) is not recommended!

Weeknight-Easy Chicken Sausage Orecchiette

Like a lot of people, many of my meal ideas come from just looking in the fridge, seeing what I've got, and making something of it. So when Ed showed up with chicken sausage one day, that's exactly what I did. Now this is one of our favorite pasta dishes. I really love how all of the flavors complement one another.

Serves: 4 to 5   **Prep Time: 15 min**   **Cook Time: 25 min**

1 pound orecchiette pasta

2 tablespoons olive oil

1 onion, chopped

3 cloves garlic, minced

1 (12-ounce) package Italian-style smoked chicken sausage, cut into ¼-inch slices

2 tablespoons finely chopped fresh sage

1 pound Brussels sprouts, trimmed and thinly sliced

1 cup chicken broth

1 teaspoon red pepper flakes (optional)

½ teaspoon salt

¼ teaspoon black pepper

¼ cup shredded Parmesan cheese

❖ Cook pasta according to package directions; set aside.

❖ Meanwhile, in a soup pot or large deep skillet over medium-high heat, heat oil. Sauté onion and garlic until golden. Add sausage and sage, and sauté for 2 minutes, stirring occasionally. Add Brussels sprouts and sauté until tender.

❖ Add broth, red pepper flakes, if desired, salt, black pepper, and cooked pasta; toss to combine. Heat for 3 to 4 minutes or until heated through. Sprinkle with Parmesan cheese and serve immediately.

TARA'S TIP: If you can't find orecchiette pasta in your supermarket, you can substitute with mini penne or shells.

Super-Sized Chicken Burritos

If you enjoyed eating my breakfast burritos (page 13), then you're really going to love these burritos that are good for lunch or dinner. They're big, so make sure you bring your appetite to the table. Plus, they're stuffed with a complete Tex-Mex meal, so you know you're going to walk away feeling full and satisfied. You can even wrap these up in some aluminum foil and take them to the park for an outdoor lunch.

Makes: 6   **Prep Time: 10 min**   **Cook Time: 45 min**

2 cups cooked yellow rice (see Tip)

1-½ cups shredded rotisserie chicken

1 (15-ounce) can black beans, rinsed and drained

1 cup frozen corn, thawed

1 cup shredded Mexican cheese blend

1-½ cups medium salsa, plus extra for topping

2 teaspoons cumin

1 tablespoon chopped fresh cilantro

6 (10-inch) flour tortillas

2 to 3 avocados, pitted, peeled, and sliced

- Preheat oven to 375 degrees F. Coat a rimmed 13- x 9-inch Lid-It or baking sheet with cooking spray.

- In a large bowl, combine all ingredients except tortillas and avocado; mix well.

- Place tortillas in the oven, directly on the rack for about 1 minute or until warmed. (This will make them nice and flexible, so rolling them will be a breeze.)

- Spoon mixture evenly onto center of each tortilla. Fold bottom of tortilla over the filling and pull back gently. Fold right side in, then repeat with the left side and roll up. Place each burrito seam-side down on Lid-It and cover with aluminum foil.

- Bake for 45 to 50 minutes or until heated through. Serve with sliced avocado.

TARA'S TIP: Rotisserie chicken is one of my favorite shortcuts. It saves so much time and one chicken can usually be used for a couple of different recipes! And rather than cooking the yellow rice for these, a lot of times I just pick up a package of cooked yellow rice in the grocery store. You can find it right next to the uncooked rice and it sure is a time saver!

Crazy Cantina Chicken Casserole

I'm all about one-dish cooking (that's one of the reasons why I came up with temptations!), and this casserole is a one-dish wonder. It's great for mid-week, when you know you're going to need a little bit of a cooking break. You can also prepare it the night before and just heat it up when you get home from work or picking the kids up from school.

Serves: 4 to 5   **Prep Time: 5 min**   **Cook Time: 35 min**

3 cups diced cooked chicken

1 cup cooked white rice

1 (10-¾-ounce) can condensed cream of chicken soup

1 (14-½-ounce) can diced tomatoes, drained

1 cup frozen corn

2 teaspoons taco seasoning mix

1-½ cups shredded pepper jack cheese, divided

1 cup corn chips, coarsely broken

- Preheat oven to 350 degrees F. Coat a 2-quart baking dish with cooking spray.

- In a large bowl, combine chicken, rice, soup, tomatoes, corn, taco seasoning, and 1 cup cheese; mix well. Spoon into baking dish. Sprinkle corn chips over top.

- Bake for 30 to 35 minutes or until center is bubbling hot. Sprinkle with remaining ½ cup cheese and bake for an additional 5 minutes or until the cheese is melted. Serve and enjoy.

TARA'S TIP: If you're putting this together the night before, I suggest putting the corn chips on right before you're going to bake it. Otherwise, they might get a little soggy in the fridge.

Unwrapped Chicken Cordon Bleu

Traditionally, chicken cordon bleu has all the ham and cheese wrapped up inside the chicken. But I don't think traditional is always the best or easiest way to go. So I changed things up by layering all of the inside goodness on top of the chicken and smothering it with a creamy sauce. To make it even better, I finish it off with a crunchy, buttery topping.

Makes: 4   **Prep Time: 10 min**   **Cook Time: 35 min**

4 boneless, skinless chicken breasts (about 2 pounds total)

⅓ pound thinly sliced deli ham

8 slices Swiss cheese

1 (10-¾-ounce) can condensed cream of chicken soup

½ cup dry white wine

1 cup herb-seasoned stuffing mix

½ stick butter, melted

- Preheat oven to 350 degrees F. Coat a rimmed 13- x 9-inch Lid-It or baking sheet with cooking spray.

- Place chicken on the Lid-It. Evenly divide ham slices on top of chicken, making sure to fold the slices so they have height to them. Top each with 2 slices of cheese.

- In a small bowl, mix together soup and wine; pour over cheese. In another small bowl, combine stuffing mix with butter. Sprinkle the stuffing mix over the sauce.

- Bake for 35 to 40 minutes or until chicken is cooked through and no pink remains.

TARA'S TIP: If you prefer not to add the wine, you can replace it with water. But, if you love wine like I do, go ahead and pour yourself a glass and enjoy it with dinner!

Chicken Parmesan Burgers

I'll be honest with you—I don't think ground chicken is all that exciting. A lot of times, it just lacks flavor. But I found a way to make it work, and I did it by recreating a yummy Italian dish! To make sure my patties are really flavorful, I mix the ground chicken with lots of seasonings. Then I go ahead and top it with all that other good stuff (the cheese and sauce). Yes, it's unexpected, but it's also really delicious!

Makes: 4 **Prep Time: 10 min** **Cook Time: 15 min**

1 pound ground chicken

1 tablespoon chopped fresh basil, plus extra for sprinkling

1 tablespoon grated Parmesan cheese

1 teaspoon Italian seasoning

½ teaspoon garlic powder

½ teaspoon salt

¼ teaspoon black pepper

½ cup Italian-style panko bread crumbs

1 tablespoon olive oil

1 cup spaghetti sauce

4 slices mozzarella cheese

1 French bread, cut into 4 sections diagonally, then cut in half lengthwise

In a large bowl, combine chicken, 1 tablespoon basil, the Parmesan cheese, Italian seasoning, garlic powder, salt, and pepper; mix just until combined. Form mixture into 4 patties.

Place bread crumbs in a shallow dish. Coat burgers evenly in bread crumbs on both sides.

In a skillet over medium heat, heat oil until hot. Place breaded burgers in skillet and cook for 8 to 12 minutes or until no longer pink in center, turning them halfway through cooking. Top each burger with a spoonful of spaghetti sauce and a slice of mozzarella cheese. Cover pan and heat for 2 to 3 minutes or until cheese is melted.

Place burger on bread, sprinkle with additional basil, and top with remaining bread; serve.

TARA'S TIP: For picture-perfect cheese, add a few tablespoons of water to the skillet before placing the lid on it. This will create steam and melt the cheese perfectly.

Lemony Chicken Skillet

Dinner in under a half hour—who's on board?! If you got excited, then wait till you bite into this light-tasting and flavorful chicken dish. Chicken breasts are so easy to cook, and with a flavor-packed sauce like this one, you really can't go wrong. I suggest a side of orzo with this. It'll soak up sauce, so you don't miss out on any of the buttery lemon goodness.

Makes: 6   **Prep Time: 15 min**   **Cook Time: 10 min**

⅔ cup all-purpose flour

½ teaspoon salt

¼ teaspoon black pepper

¾ stick butter, divided

6 boneless, skinless chicken breasts, pounded to ¼-inch thickness

½ cup dry white wine

Juice of 2 lemons (about 4 tablespoons)

1 tablespoon chopped fresh parsley

2 tablespoons capers (optional)

- In a shallow dish, combine flour, salt, and pepper; mix well.

- In a large skillet over medium heat, melt 1 tablespoon butter. Coat chicken evenly with flour mixture; increase temperature to medium-high heat and sauté chicken, in batches, for 2 to 3 minutes per side or until golden, adding more butter as needed. Remove to a plate and keep warm.

- Add wine, lemon juice, parsley, remaining butter, and the capers, if desired, to the skillet; mix well. Return chicken to skillet and cook for 3 to 4 minutes or until sauce begins to thicken. Serve chicken topped with lemony sauce.

Lancaster County Chicken Casserole

I live near the Amish country, right by Lancaster County, so I've had my fair share of Amish cooking. This casserole is inspired by their cuisine (well, maybe not the Parmesan ... I don't think I've met any Italian Amish). What you're going to find here is lots of creamy, hearty, goodness. This casserole is going to deliver a big dose of comfort.

Serves: 4 to 6   **Prep Time: 10 min**   **Cook Time: 45 min**

8 ounces medium egg noodles

1 stick butter

⅓ cup all-purpose flour

2 cups chicken broth

1 cup milk or half-and-half

1 teaspoon salt

½ teaspoon black pepper

2 cups chopped rotisserie chicken

2 cups sliced fresh mushrooms

⅓ cup thinly sliced scallions

¼ cup grated Parmesan cheese

- Cook noodles according to package directions; drain well and set aside.

- Preheat oven to 350 degrees F. Coat a 13- x 9-inch baking dish with cooking spray; set aside.

- In a medium saucepan over low heat, melt butter; gradually add flour, stirring until smooth. Cook for 1 minute or until golden, stirring constantly. Gradually whisk in the chicken broth and milk; increase heat to medium and cook until mixture is slightly thickened, stirring constantly. Stir in salt and pepper; set aside.

- In a large bowl, combine cooked noodles, chicken, mushrooms, and scallions; stir in sauce. Spoon mixture into baking dish and sprinkle with Parmesan cheese.

- Bake uncovered for 25 to 30 minutes or until heated through and the top is crispy.

TARA'S TIP: This makes a lot for just two people, so when it's just Ed and me, I divide everything into 9-ounce oval ramekins. That way, I just bake a couple for dinner that night and freeze the rest for another time.

Tex-Mex Chicken Stuffed Shells

I want to get you ready to think about stuffed shells in a whole new way. So just for a second, let's forget about the Italian-style stuffed shells as you know them. Now let's imagine the shells as an empty canvas, ready to be stuffed with anything. Like maybe an entire Tex-Mex chicken feast. How does that sound? I hope you said "amazing," because that's the experience this recipe is going to deliver.

Serves: 6 to 8   **Prep Time: 10 min**   **Cook Time: 30 min**

1 (12-ounce) package jumbo shell pasta

1 (8-ounce) package cream cheese

2 cups salsa, divided

½ teaspoon garlic powder

2 cups diced cooked chicken

1 cup frozen corn, thawed

1 (15-ounce) can black beans, rinsed and drained

2 cups shredded Mexican cheese blend

❖ Preheat oven to 350 degrees F. Coat a 13- x 9-inch baking dish with cooking spray.

❖ Cook the shells according to package directions; drain and rinse well. (I found that spraying them with cooking spray helps prevent them from sticking.)

❖ In a skillet over medium-high heat, melt the cream cheese and add ½ cup salsa and the garlic powder; mix until creamy. Then gently stir in the cooked chicken, corn, and black beans until well combined.

❖ Spoon 1 cup of salsa on the bottom of the baking dish. Using a couple of soup spoons, fill the shells with chicken mixture and place them in the baking dish. (I use one spoon to scoop up the filling and the other to push it gently into the shells.) Spoon the remaining salsa over the top of the shells.

❖ Cover with foil and bake for 20 minutes. Uncover, sprinkle with cheese and bake for an additional 10 minutes or until the filling is hot and the cheese is melted. Serve immediately.

TARA'S TIP: When I make these for a crowd I usually use a medium salsa. However, when I make these for the family, the salsa gets a little bit spicier. Make sure you use whatever your crowd or family can handle!

Traditional Chicken Marsala

As you might have noticed, I like putting my own spin on things all the time. But that doesn't mean that I don't stick to traditional recipes on occasion. Chicken Marsala is one of my favorite classic Italian dishes. I love everything from the sauce to the mushrooms, and how everything comes together so easily. I make this dish at least twice a month and never get sick of it.

Serves: 4 to 5 **Prep Time: 15 min** **Cook Time: 20 min**

½ cup all-purpose flour

1 teaspoon salt

¼ teaspoon black pepper

1-½ pounds chicken cutlets

3 tablespoons butter

3 tablespoons olive oil

½ pound fresh mushrooms, sliced

2 cloves garlic, minced

¾ cup sweet Marsala wine (see Tip)

½ cup chicken broth

In a shallow dish, combine flour, salt, and pepper. Coat chicken evenly with flour mixture; set aside.

In a large skillet over medium heat, heat butter and oil. (The butter gives the chicken a rich taste and the oil prevents the butter from scorching.) Cook chicken for 2 to 3 minutes per side, in batches, if needed. Remove cooked chicken to a platter and keep warm.

Add mushrooms and garlic to skillet and sauté for 4 to 5 minutes or until tender. Return chicken to skillet, add wine and chicken broth, and reduce heat to low. Cook for 4 to 5 minutes or until sauce thickens and chicken is heated through, stirring occasionally. Spoon the sauce and mushrooms over the chicken and enjoy.

TARA'S TIP: If you've never cooked with Marsala wine, then this is the perfect recipe to try it. Unlike most cooking wines, Marsala has a sweet, nutty taste that really makes the chicken stand out. I suggest picking up a small bottle at your neighborhood liquor store and giving it a try.

Diner-Style Turkey Meatloaf

When I was growing up, everyone came to the dinner table to eat together. These days, I still feel it's important to keep this tradition going. Sharing our day over a home-cooked meal certainly has brought my family closer together. If it's been some time since your entire family has gathered around the table, I suggest cooking up this comforting turkey meatloaf and inviting everyone over.

Serves: 4 to 6   **Prep Time: 5 min**   **Cook Time: 55 min**

2 pounds ground turkey

½ cup Italian-style bread crumbs

¾ cup chopped onion

3 cloves garlic, minced

1 tablespoon Worcestershire sauce

1 egg

¼ cup water

½ teaspoon salt

¼ teaspoon black pepper

¾ cup ketchup, divided

- Preheat oven to 350 degrees F. Coat a 1.5-quart loaf pan with cooking spray.

- In a large bowl, combine turkey, bread crumbs, onion, garlic, Worcestershire sauce, egg, water, salt, pepper, and ½ cup ketchup; mix well. Place mixture in pan and pat down gently.

- Bake for 40 minutes, then spread remaining ¼ cup ketchup over top. Return to oven and bake for 15 more minutes or until no pink remains and juices run clear. Let rest for 5 minutes before slicing and serving.

TARA'S TIP: For the ultimate comforting dinner, serve this turkey meatloaf alongside mashed potatoes and homemade gravy, if time permits. For a shortcut, a store-bought gravy will do the trick.

Pecan-Crusted Turkey Cutlets

On Thanksgiving, it's pretty common to see turkey and pecans on the same dinner table, but you don't really see that combo other times of the year. Well I'm going to put a change to that! Once you try my pecan-crusted turkey, you might just find yourself making this dish year-round. The pecans add a light buttery crunch that's pretty irresistible.

Makes: 4   **Prep Time: 10 min**   **Cook Time: 8 min**

½ cup pecans

¾ cup bread crumbs

¾ teaspoon salt, divided

¾ teaspoon black pepper, divided

4 thinly cut boneless turkey cutlets

⅓ cup all-purpose flour

2 large eggs, lightly beaten

3 tablespoons olive oil

- In a food processor or a blender, combine the pecans and bread crumbs until finely chopped. Place in a shallow dish.

- Season the turkey with ½ teaspoon each of salt and pepper. Combine the flour and remaining ¼ teaspoon salt and ¼ teaspoon pepper in a shallow dish. Dredge turkey cutlets in the flour mixture; dip in eggs, and coat with bread crumb mixture.

- In a large skillet over medium heat, heat oil until hot. Sauté the cutlets for 4 to 5 minutes per side or until no pink remains on the inside and they're golden on the outside. Serve as-is or drizzle with my Honey Mustard Sauce. (See Tip.)

TARA'S TIP: My Honey Mustard Sauce is super easy to make, and everyone always goes nuts for it. All you need to do is combine ½ cup mayonnaise, 3 tablespoons honey, 2 tablespoons Dijon mustard, ¼ teaspoon paprika, and ⅛ teaspoon salt. Mix it all up and you're done!

EVERY PIECE IS TESTED
over and over again
TO MAKE SURE IT'LL STAND UP
TO YOUR EVERYDAY LIFESTYLE.

Marvelous Meat

Special Occasion Stuffed Flank Steak

During the holidays, I do a lot of entertaining—I mean, A LOT. And when people come over, I like to show off a little bit. (Who doesn't?) This is one of my go-to recipes for dropping jaws around the dinner table. It's everyday easy, but tastes and looks holiday special. Serve it with a side of crispy, oven-roasted potatoes and enjoy a totally delicious dinner.

Serves: 4 to 6   **Prep Time: 20 min**   **Cook Time: 1 hr**

1 (2-pound) flank steak

Salt for sprinkling

Black pepper for sprinkling

Garlic powder for sprinkling

2 cups (4 ounces) fresh spinach

6 slices (4 ounces) provolone cheese

½ cup roasted red pepper strips, drained well

❖ Preheat oven to 350 degrees F. Coat a rimmed Lid-It or baking sheet with cooking spray.

❖ Before stuffing the steak, you'll need to butterfly it. To butterfly, place steak on a cutting board and rest one hand on top of it. Using your other hand, with a sharp slicing knife and holding your knife parallel to the cutting board, carefully cut steak in half about ¾ of the way through. When you're done, it should open up like a book. Generously sprinkle both sides with salt, black pepper, and garlic powder.

❖ With steak "opened up", place spinach over steak; then top evenly with cheese. Place pepper strips down center, lengthwise. Starting from the shortest side, roll steak up jelly roll-style. Secure it with toothpicks or tie it with butcher string, and place seam-side down on Lid-It.

❖ Roast for 1 hour or until internal temperature registers 135 degrees for medium rare or until desired doneness. Let rest for 10 minutes before slicing. Remove toothpicks or string before serving.

TARA'S TIP: This goes great with homemade pesto sauce! To make it, combine ½ cup olive oil, ½ cup loosely packed fresh basil, ¼ teaspoon salt, ¼ teaspoon black pepper, and 8 cloves garlic in a mini chopper or blender until smooth.

Gail's Slow Roasted Brisket

This is one of two brisket recipes I grew up eating. My mom, Gail, would make this in her slow cooker. She'd toss everything in and kind of forget about it while it cooked. I've found that it's just as easy slow roasting a brisket in the oven, especially when the roast is on the bigger side. Whichever way you choose, you'll end up with an all-American meal that's a real winner.

Serves: 8 to 10　　　**Prep Time: 10 min**　　　**Cook Time: 3-½ hrs**

1 (4- to 6-pound) beef brisket

2 (10-½-ounce) cans condensed onion soup

1 (14-ounce) can whole berry cranberry sauce

2 large onions, thinly sliced

❖ Preheat oven to 350 degrees F. Coat a large roasting pan with cooking spray; place brisket in the pan fat-side up.

❖ In a medium bowl, combine onion soup and cranberry sauce; mix well. Pour over brisket, then top with sliced onions.

❖ Cover tightly and roast for 3-½ to 4 hours or until the meat is fork-tender. Slice across the grain and serve topped with sauce from pan.

TARA'S TIP: If you prefer to make this in a slow cooker, place the brisket in a 6-quart or larger slow cooker. Add the onion soup and cranberry sauce mixture, then top with onions. Cook on LOW for 8 to 9 hours or until the meat is fork-tender.

Steak & Veggie Stir-Fry

When I think of the ultimate one-pan meal, the first thing I think of is stir-fry. It's quick and easy to prepare, and cleanup is a breeze! Plus, you can customize it with whatever veggies you have on hand. And when you lace it with my throw-together Asian Ginger Sauce, all the better. I like to serve this over a bed of fragrant rice, like jasmine or basmati.

Serves: 4 to 6   Prep Time: 10 min   Cook Time: 8 min

Asian Ginger Sauce

½ cup beef broth

3 tablespoons soy sauce

1 tablespoon cornstarch

1 teaspoon ground ginger

2 tablespoons peanut oil

1 red bell pepper, cut into strips

2 cups sliced
fresh mushrooms

1 cup sliced scallions

1 clove garlic, minced

1 (1 to 1-½ pound) bottom
round steak, cut into
¼-inch strips

To make the Asian Ginger Sauce, in a small bowl, combine broth, soy sauce, cornstarch, and ginger; mix well and set aside.

In a large skillet or wok over high heat, heat oil until hot. Add bell pepper, mushrooms, scallions, and garlic, and cook for 4 to 5 minutes or until vegetables are tender, stirring occasionally. Add steak and sauté for 2 to 3 additional minutes or until browned.

Add sauce to skillet and cook for 2 to 3 minutes or until it thickens, stirring frequently.

Sirloin & Scallops with Béarnaise Sauce

Think of this as an easy weeknight version of surf and turf. The Béarnaise sauce gives it a little extra somethin' that really makes it wow-worthy. Not to mention, you're getting rich-tasting, buttery, sea scallops and juicy slices of steak. It's a good thing I didn't include a picture of this one or you might've drooled right on the page.

Serves: 4　　　**Prep Time: 10 min**　　　**Cook Time: 20 min**

1 (.9-ounce) packet Béarnaise sauce

1 (10- to 12-ounce) sirloin or strip steak

1 teaspoon kosher salt, divided

½ teaspoon black pepper, divided

½ teaspoon garlic powder

3 tablespoons butter, divided

12 sea scallops

❖ Prepare Béarnaise sauce according to packet directions; keep warm.

❖ Evenly sprinkle steak with ½ teaspoon kosher salt, ¼ teaspoon pepper, and the garlic powder.

❖ In a medium skillet over medium-high heat, melt 1 tablespoon butter; cook steak for 4 to 5 minutes per side or until desired doneness. Remove steak to a cutting board and let rest.

❖ Wipe skillet with a paper towel (be careful, it will still be warm). In the same skillet, over medium heat, melt remaining 2 tablespoons butter. Sprinkle scallops with remaining ½ teaspoon salt and ¼ teaspoon pepper, and sauté for 3 to 4 minutes per side or until golden and firm in center.

❖ Cut steak, across the grain, into 12 slices and place on a platter. Top each slice with a scallop; spoon Béarnaise sauce over steak and scallops.

TARA'S TIP: Don't use bay scallops in this recipe—they're too small and tend to get rubbery. You get a lot more bang for your buck with the larger sea scallops, since they're nice and meaty.

Swedish Meatballs Over Noodles

I've been eating these meatballs since I was six years old. One holiday season, my mom's best friend, who was Swedish, taught her how to make them. Since then, they've been a holiday tradition in our house. My mom's friend has now passed, but we continue to make these in remembrance of her, and serve them with lingonberry jam just like she did. This recipe holds a special place in my heart.

Serves: 6 to 8   **Prep Time: 20 min**   **Cook Time: 30 min**

1 pound ground beef

1 pound ground pork

1 small onion, grated

1 cup plain bread crumbs

2 eggs, beaten

1 tablespoon Worcestershire sauce

1-½ teaspoons salt

1 teaspoon ground nutmeg

1 teaspoon black pepper

2 tablespoon butter

1 tablespoon olive oil

¼ cup all-purpose flour

2 cups beef stock

½ cup sour cream

1 (12-ounce) package wide egg noodles, cooked according to package directions

Chopped parsley for sprinkling

❖ Preheat oven to 350 degrees F.

❖ In a large bowl, combine beef and pork, onion, bread crumbs, eggs, Worcestershire sauce, salt, nutmeg, and pepper; gently mix until well combined. (Don't over-handle mixture or it'll make your meatballs tough.)

❖ Roll mixture into 1-inch meatballs and place them on rimmed 13- x 9- inch Lid-Its or baking sheets. Bake 20 to 22 minutes or until no pink remains in meatballs.

❖ Meanwhile, in a large skillet over medium heat, heat butter and olive oil. When butter is melted, whisk in flour and cook until golden. Slowly whisk in beef stock, stirring until sauce thickens.

❖ Add meatballs to skillet, and simmer for 5 minutes. Gently stir in sour cream, being careful that you don't break up the meatballs. Spoon meatballs and sauce over noodles. Sprinkle with parsley and serve.

Not-Your-Routine Poutine Burgers

I wanted to get on board with the poutine craze, so I whipped up an easy version of a poutine burger that can best be described as perfection. Not only is this easy and fun, but I stand firm in my belief that everything is better with french fries. Wait till you sink your teeth into this one!

Makes: 4   **Prep Time: 10 min**   **Cook Time: 20 min**

1-½ pounds ground beef

2 tablespoons water

1 tablespoon steak seasoning

½ (32-ounce) package frozen shoestring french fries

1 (12-ounce) jar beef gravy

4 kaiser rolls, split

1 (12-ounce) package cheese curds

In a large bowl, combine ground beef, water, and steak seasoning; mix just until combined. Shape mixture into 4 equal-sized burgers. Place an indentation in center of each burger with your thumb. (This keeps it from swelling up in the middle and helps it cook evenly.)

Prepare the french fries according to package directions. In a small saucepan over medium heat, heat gravy until hot; reduce heat to keep warm.

Meanwhile, heat a large skillet or grill pan over medium-high heat or preheat your grill to medium high and cook the burgers 4 to 5 minutes per side or until desired doneness.

Place burgers onto the bottom halves of rolls. Pile the french fries evenly on each burger and top with cheese curds. Drizzle gravy over cheese and fries and place top halves of rolls on each one. Serve immediately.

TARA'S TIP: I like to serve this with, with what I call a "side car" of gravy. That way, you can drizzle on more beef goodness as you go.

Mexican Rolled Meatloaf

When it comes to meatloaf, I'm pretty sure there isn't a combo of spices and add-ins that hasn't been tested. And I'm guessing you have at least one or two basic meatloaf recipes that you go to all the time. So rather than simply sharing a "me too" meatloaf, I decided to share one that always gets rave reviews. It's a rolled-up version that features lots of yummy Mexican flavors. I hope you enjoy it as much as I do!

Serves: 6 to 8   **Prep Time: 15 min**   **Cook Time: 55 min**

1 pound ground beef

1 pound ground pork

3 slices white bread, torn into small pieces

2 eggs

1-¼ cups salsa, divided

1 teaspoon salt

⅛ teaspoon black pepper

2 cups (8 ounces) shredded pepper jack cheese

- Preheat oven to 350 degrees F. Coat a 13- x 9-inch baking dish with cooking spray.

- In a large bowl, combine beef and pork, bread, eggs, ¼ cup salsa, salt, and pepper. Mix with your hands until well blended. Place on a 12- x 15-inch piece of wax paper and form into a 10- x 12-inch rectangle, about ½-inch thick.

- Sprinkle cheese evenly over meat mixture. Roll up jelly roll-style, starting from the short end, by lifting wax paper and removing the paper as you roll. Pinch the seam together to seal. Place seam-side down in baking dish.

- Spoon ½ cup of salsa over roll and roast for 45 minutes. Remove from oven, spoon remaining ½ cup of salsa over roll, and return to oven for 10 to 15 minutes or until no pink remains. Remove from oven and allow to rest for 10 minutes. Slice and serve.

Killer Chili Baked Potatoes

I'm all about comfort food, so obviously, chili is always a top choice. You can serve this as a hearty dinner or make mini versions using smaller baked potatoes for a football-watching party. Since everyone loves adding their own toppings, I always put out bowls of sour cream, shredded cheddar, and scallions so everyone can help themselves.

Makes: 4   **Prep Time: 5 min**   **Cook Time: 55 min**

4 large russet baking potatoes

1 pound ground beef

¾ cup chopped onion

2 cloves garlic, minced

1 (14-ounce) can crushed tomatoes

1 (16-ounce) can red kidney beans, drained

3 tablespoons chili powder

½ teaspoon ground cumin

½ teaspoon salt

½ teaspoon black pepper

∴ Preheat oven to 400 degrees F. Scrub potatoes and pierce skins with a fork. Bake for 55 minutes or until tender. (This time will vary based on the size of your potatoes.)

∴ Meanwhile, in a large pot over medium-high heat, sauté beef, onion, and garlic for 8 to 10 minutes or until no pink remains in the beef; drain off excess liquid.

∴ Add remaining ingredients; mix well. Cover, reduce heat to low, and simmer for 45 minutes, stirring occasionally.

∴ Cut a slit in the top of each potato and gently push the ends of the potato together so that it opens up. Spoon chili inside the slit. Serve immediately with any additional chili on the side.

TARA'S TIP: I switch up my chili all the time. Sometimes I use beef—other times, I go for turkey. You can even try it with different kinds of beans. If you find yourself with any leftovers, just place them in an airtight container in the freezer. The chili freezes well and can easily be reheated for a hearty meal on a busy weeknight..

Luck-of-the-Irish Shepherd's Pie

My dad loved shepherd's pie, so much so that my mom would make it quite a bit when we were growing up. She wasn't too particular about the recipe so it would often morph into a bunch of different things, but I thought I'd keep it traditional with this one. I suggest telling everyone to come to the table with an empty stomach, because, between the potatoes and beefy veggie goodness, this one is really hearty.

Serves: 4 to 6   **Prep Time: 10 min**   **Cook Time: 30 min**

5 tablespoons butter, divided

1 large onion, diced

2 cups thinly sliced carrots

1-¼ pounds ground beef or ground lamb

½ teaspoon dried thyme

¾ teaspoon black pepper, divided

2 tablespoons all-purpose flour

½ cup beef broth

2 tablespoons tomato paste

1 cup frozen peas

2 pounds russet potatoes, cut into chunks

1 teaspoon salt

2 tablespoons milk

- Preheat oven to 400 degrees F.

- In a large skillet over medium-high heat, melt 1 tablespoon butter. Sauté onion and carrots for 7 to 8 minutes or until tender. Add beef, thyme, and ½ teaspoon black pepper. Cook for 6 to 8 minutes or until no pink remains in the beef, stirring to crumble. Add flour and stir to combine; let simmer for about 1 minute.

- Add broth and tomato paste, then cook for 3 to 4 minutes or until liquid reduces slightly. Stir in peas and simmer for 1 minute. Place mixture into 4 mini-bakers (as shown) or in a 1.5-quart casserole dish.

- Meanwhile, in a large saucepan, place potatoes in enough water to cover. Over high heat, bring to a boil and cook for 15 minutes or until tender; drain well. Return potatoes to pot and add remaining 4 tablespoons butter, remaining ¼ teaspoon black pepper, and the milk. Beat with an electric mixer until smooth and creamy.

- Spoon or pipe the mashed potatoes over the meat mixture. Bake for about 20 minutes or until mashed potatoes are golden and meat mixture is piping hot.

Sausage Stuffed Peppers

You should know that I'm crazy about stuffed peppers. I love how each one is the perfect portion for one person and I love how they look when you mix and match different colored peppers. I also love the crunch that the pepper adds (which is why it's important not to overcook them). Plus, these are stuffed with sausage, another one of my loves! I can't wait for you to fall in love with these too.

Makes: 6

Prep Time: 15 min

Cook Time: 55 min

1 (24-ounce) jar spaghetti sauce, divided

2 pounds bulk mild Italian sausage

1-½ cups uncooked instant rice

2 cups shredded mozzarella cheese, divided

3/4 cup water

6 medium bell peppers, tops removed, and seeded

⁙ Preheat oven to 375 degrees F. Spread 1 cup spaghetti sauce on bottom of a 13- x 9-inch baking dish.

⁙ In a large bowl, combine sausage, rice, 1-½ cups cheese, 1-¼ cups spaghetti sauce, and the water; mix well.

⁙ Stuff each pepper with an equal amount of mixture and place in baking dish. Pour remaining sauce evenly over peppers.

⁙ Cover and cook for 50 to 60 minutes or until no pink remains in sausage and rice is tender. Uncover and sprinkle with remaining ½ cup cheese. Bake for 5 more minutes or until cheese is melted. Spoon sauce from pan over peppers and serve.

Italian Roasted Ribs with Cherry Peppers

Guys, I think I outdid myself with this one! These ribs are based off of one of my favorite dishes that I order whenever I go to this pretty popular Italian restaurant. I decided to recreate them at home, and I have to say ... they might even be better than the restaurant's version. They're a little tangy, a little sweet, and so aromatic. Now I can have as much as I want without attracting any attention—yum!

Serves: 4 to 5   **Prep Time: 10 min**   **Cook Time: 60 min**

1 tablespoon chopped fresh rosemary

1-½ teaspoons salt

1-½ teaspoons black pepper

4 cloves garlic, chopped

3 pounds St. Louis-style pork spare ribs

1 cup pickled cherry peppers, seeded and sliced

¼ cup pickled cherry pepper juice

¾ cup dry white wine

- Preheat oven to 375 degrees F.

- In a small bowl, mix together rosemary, salt, black pepper, and garlic; massage this rub over ribs. Place ribs on a rimmed 13- x 9-inch Lid-It or baking sheet and cover with foil.

- Roast ribs for 40 minutes. Uncover and roast for 15 more minutes or until ribs are browned and cooked through. Sprinkle with sliced cherry peppers. Pour cherry pepper juice and wine over top. Place Lid-It or baking sheet back in oven for 5 more minutes. Serve ribs with peppers and pan juices.

TARA'S TIP: Sometimes, I ask Ed to throw these on the grill right after they come out of the oven. It adds a smokiness to them, which makes them even more delicious.

Slow Cooker
Pork & Cabbage

Here's a meal that's good for your wallet and your taste buds. There's nothing fancy about it, but the combo of pork and cabbage is classically delicious. My favorite part is when it's all done—you reach into your slow cooker and the pork just falls apart. I've even convinced some non-cabbage lovers to eat this (and they've liked it!).

Serves: 6 to 8   **Prep Time: 15 min**   **Cook Time: 5 hrs**

4 cups coarsely shredded cabbage

2 apples, coarsely chopped

1 small onion, chopped

½ cup brown sugar

½ cup apple cider vinegar

½ cup apple juice

1 teaspoon salt, divided

1 (3-pound) boneless pork butt

¼ teaspoon black pepper

1 tablespoon vegetable oil

:: In a 5-quart or larger slow cooker, combine cabbage, apples, onion, sugar, vinegar, apple juice, and ½ teaspoon salt; mix well.

:: Evenly sprinkle roast with remaining ½ teaspoon salt and the pepper. In a large skillet over high heat, heat oil until hot; brown roast on all sides. Place roast in slow cooker, fat side up, on top of cabbage mixture.

:: Cover and cook on LOW for 5 to 6 hours or until pork is cooked to at least medium and is fork-tender.

TARA'S TIP: As tempting as it might be, I recommend you don't peek into your slow cooker while it's cooking. Every time you do, the slow cooker loses about 75% of its heat, which can mess with your overall cooking time.

Herb Roasted Lamb with Mint Sauce

As much as I love lamb, I don't get a chance to make it as often as I would like. But when I do, I try to team it up with fresh herbs. With an herb crust and a decadent 3-ingredient mint sauce, this lamb recipe is truly special. Serve it along with some fresh veggies and get ready for a real treat.

Serves: 4 to 6

Prep Time: 10 min

Cook Time: 45 min

2 tablespoons olive oil

½ teaspoon onion powder

½ teaspoon garlic powder

1 teaspoon salt

½ teaspoon black pepper

2 teaspoons chopped fresh rosemary

2 racks of lamb (about 2-½ pounds)

Mint Sauce

1 cup mint jelly

½ cup red wine

1 teaspoon chopped fresh rosemary

- Preheat oven to 325 degrees F. Coat a rimmed 13- x 9-inch Lid-It or baking sheet with cooking spray.

- In a small bowl, combine oil, onion powder, garlic powder, salt, pepper, and 2 teaspoons rosemary; mix well. Rub mixture evenly over lamb and place on Lid-It.

- Roast lamb for 45 minutes for medium-rare or until desired doneness.

- Meanwhile, to make Mint Sauce, in a small saucepan over low heat, combine jelly, wine, and 1 teaspoon rosemary, and simmer for 6 to 8 minutes or until jelly is melted and mixture is slightly thickened.

- Cut lamb between the ribs and serve with warmed sauce.

Slow & Saucy Pork Tacos

Tacos are the way to my heart. If I had any say in it, Taco Tuesday would last the whole week. If you feel the same way about tacos as I do, then you're going to love these. By making the pork in the slow cooker, you'll not only end up with really tender meat, but your whole house will smell amazing by the time it's done. I also love how saucy these are!

Serves: 8 to 10   **Prep Time: 10 min**   **Cook Time: 5 hrs**

2 onions, chopped

4 cloves garlic, minced

2 tablespoons chili powder

1 tablespoon ground cumin

1 (16-ounce) bottle taco sauce

1 (5- to 6-pound) boneless pork butt

10 extra-large crunchy taco shells

⁚⁚ In a medium bowl, combine onions, garlic, chili powder, cumin, and taco sauce; mix well. Place pork in a 5-quart or larger slow cooker. Pour onion mixture over top of pork.

⁚⁚ Cook on HIGH for 5 to 6 hours or on LOW for 8 to 9 hours or until pork is fall-apart tender.

⁚⁚ Remove pork to a cutting board and shred with 2 forks. While shredding, discard any pieces of fat that you come across. Place pork back into slow cooker and mix with sauce. Divide shredded pork into taco shells. Add as little or as much sauce as you like to give your tacos the perfect level of sauciness.

TARA'S TIP: Set out everyone's favorite taco toppings by using one of my temp-tations muffin pans. For starters, I suggest shredded lettuce, tomatoes, shredded cheese, olives, sliced jalapeños, and chopped cilantro.

Easy Cuban Sandwich Bake

The Cuban sandwich is my favorite sandwich. If it's on the menu, I'm ordering it (and I'm totally having it with the pickles!). Since Cuban bread isn't always easy to find, I came up with an inspired version that I could serve to my family. The very first time I made this, everyone practically cheered. Based on that, and on all my personal taste tests (and there've been many), I'll tell ya—this one is a real winner.

Serves: 4 to 6 **Prep Time: 15 min** **Cook Time: 30 min**

1 (8-ounce) package refrigerated crescent rolls

½ pound thinly sliced deli ham

½ pound thinly sliced deli roast pork

½ pound sliced Swiss cheese

2 tablespoons yellow mustard

15 dill pickle chips, drained, plus extra for garnish

1 egg, lightly beaten

❖ Preheat oven to 350 degrees F.

❖ On a flat surface, unroll crescent roll dough, pressing seams together. Separate dough into 2 squares along center-cut line. Place 1 square into an 8-inch square baking dish; using your fingertips, press the dough into the bottom of the dish.

❖ Layer with half the ham, half the pork, and half the cheese. Spread mustard evenly over cheese. Layer evenly with pickle chips. Repeat with remaining ham, pork, and cheese. Place remaining dough on top and brush with egg.

❖ Bake for 30 to 35 minutes or until golden and heated through. Let cool for 5 minutes. Cut into squares, garnish with additional pickle chips, and serve.

Drunken Orange Holiday Ham

Whether you need a great ham recipe for Easter, Christmas, or just because, I've got you covered. This ham has a citrusy-sweet taste that's made even better by the addition of a little bourbon or whiskey. So far, everyone I've served this to has loved it and they always comment on how unique it is. Of course, I take that as the ultimate compliment!

Serves: 8 to 10   **Prep Time: 10 min**   **Cook Time: 90 min**

1 (4- to 5-pound) fully cooked, semi-boneless ham

1 orange, cut into thick slices

Drunken Orange Glaze

1 cup orange marmalade

½ cup honey

⅓ cup bourbon or cinnamon whiskey

½ teaspoon vanilla extract

- Preheat oven to 325 degrees F.

- With a sharp knife, cut a diamond pattern into skin/fat layer of ham, about ½-inch deep, and place on a roasting rack in a large roasting pan. Arrange orange slices around ham.

- To make Drunken Orange Glaze, in a microwave-safe bowl, combine remaining ingredients; mix well. Heat in the microwave for about 1 minute or until warm.

- Brush about ⅓ glaze over ham and roast for 30 minutes. Baste occasionally with remaining glaze and continue to roast for about 60 more minutes or until heated through. (If ham starts to get too brown, cover roasting pan.) Let ham rest for 10 minutes before slicing. Serve with pan drippings.

FROM DAY ONE
I MADE SURE THAT
every piece
IS FREEZER, OVEN,
MICROWAVE &
DISHWASHER SAFE.

Scrumptious Seafood, Pasta, & More

One-Pan Shrimp Fajitas

Not all Mexican food has to be smothered in cheese and sour cream! When I need a healthier option to satisfy my South-of-the-Border cravings, I make fajitas. Just because they're lower in calories doesn't mean you're going to miss out on any flavor. And if you're craving an extra burst of "Yum!" just squeeze on some lime and sprinkle on some chopped cilantro.

Serves: 4   **Prep Time: 10 min**   **Cook Time: 25 min**

1 red bell pepper, cut into ½-inch strips

1 green bell pepper, cut into ½-inch strips

1 onion, cut into ½-inch strips

2 tablespoons vegetable oil, divided

1 (1-ounce) package taco seasoning mix, divided

1 pound medium shrimp, peeled, deveined, and tails removed

8 (6-inch) flour tortillas

- Preheat oven to 425 degrees F.

- In a large bowl, combine peppers, onion, 1 tablespoon oil, and ½ package taco seasoning mix; mix until vegetables are evenly coated. Place vegetables on a rimmed 13- x 9-inch Lid-It or baking sheet. Roast for 20 minutes.

- Meanwhile, place shrimp in same bowl, add remaining 1 tablespoon oil and remaining taco seasoning mix; mix well. Arrange shrimp on top of cooked veggies.

- Roast for 5 to 7 more minutes or until shrimp turn pink and are cooked through. Wrap tortillas in foil and place in oven during the last 5 minutes of cooking. Serve the shrimp and veggies folded in the warmed tortillas and enjoy.

Mango-Tango
Fish Taco Cups

I love making these in the summertime! These little fish cups are so cute and deliver a fresh taste that reminds me a lot of something you might eat on a tropical getaway. The sweet and citrusy mango salsa complements the cumin-spiced mahi-mahi perfectly. Make this for guests or whenever you want something light and flavor-packed to enjoy poolside.

Makes: 6   Prep Time: 15 min   Cook Time: 20 min   Chill Time: 2 hrs

Mango Salsa

1 ripe mango, pitted, peeled, and chopped

¼ cup chopped green bell pepper

¼ cup chopped red bell pepper

¼ cup chopped red onion

2 tablespoons orange juice

2 tablespoons lime juice

2 tablespoons honey

1 tablespoon chopped fresh cilantro

¼ teaspoon salt

6 (6-inch) flour tortillas

¼ teaspoon ground cumin

¼ teaspoon salt

1 tablespoon olive oil

1 pound mahi-mahi or other firm white fish

1-½ cups shredded romaine lettuce

:: In a medium bowl, combine all Mango Salsa ingredients; mix well. Cover and refrigerate for at least 2 hours before serving.

:: Preheat oven to 350 degrees F. Place tortillas directly on oven racks and warm 1 minute. While still warm, place a tortilla over the bottom of a small juice glass that you've turned upside-down on your counter (the bottom of the glass should be about 2 inches across). Make sure the tortilla is centered on the glass. Gently form each tortilla over the bottom of the glass; invert the glass and tortilla and use the glass to gently place the tortilla into each cup of a muffin pan. Repeat with remaining tortillas. Place muffin pan in the oven and bake for 5 minutes or until crisp. Remove from oven and set aside.

:: Meanwhile, in a small bowl, combine cumin, remaining ¼ teaspoon salt, and the olive oil. Place fish into an 8-inch square baking dish and brush both sides with oil mixture. Bake for 18 to 20 minutes or until fish flakes easily with a fork.

:: Divide lettuce evenly into tortilla cups. Break fish into bite-sized pieces (the fish can be served hot or cold) and place on top of lettuce. Top with Mango Salsa and serve. Spoon the juice of the salsa over each cup for even more flavor.

Old-Fashioned Shrimp Boil

Shrimp boils are a hallmark of summer and an old-fashioned pastime that I love. Once you've got everything cooked, just dump it all out on some newspaper and let everybody have at it. It's always fun to see friends and family rushing for their favorites! If you haven't had this experience at least once in your life, I suggest you find a picnic table and get going!

Serves: 3 to 4   **Prep Time: 10 min**   **Cook Time: 25 min**

8 cups water

2 tablespoons seafood seasoning (I use Old Bay®.)

½ teaspoon salt

¼ teaspoon cayenne pepper (optional)

1 pound kielbasa sausage, cut into 2-inch pieces

6 red potatoes, cut in half

2 onions, peeled and cut in quarters

3 ears corn, cut into 3-inch pieces

1 pound large shrimp, unpeeled

❖ In a soup pot, combine water, seafood seasoning, salt, and cayenne pepper, if desired. Bring to a boil over high heat, then add sausage, potatoes, onions, and corn.

❖ Cook for 15 to 20 minutes or until potatoes are fork-tender. Add shrimp and cook 2 to 3 more minutes or until shrimp are pink and cooked through.

❖ Strain and reserve broth. Serve sausage, shrimp, and veggies immediately, along with the broth for dunking.

TARA'S TIP: This recipe easily doubles or triples depending on the size of your party. Also, this is a great time to dig out those ramekins! You can use them to give everyone their own cup of broth for dunking.

Wined and Dined Tuscan Clams

A handful of good Italian ingredients really helps to take this clam dish to the next level. Since the tomato sauce makes this almost stew-like, I like serving it over a light pasta, like angel hair. It's also great with some crusty bread! If you're a fan of mussels, you can even do this with a half-and-half mix. Either way, I think you'll find that this dish is pretty unforgettable.

Serves: 3 to 4   **Prep Time: 5 min**   **Cook Time: 10 min**

4 dozen littleneck clams

1 (14-½-ounce) can stewed tomatoes, chopped, with juice reserved

2 cloves garlic

½ cup dry white wine

2 tablespoons chopped fresh basil

¼ teaspoon black pepper

❖ In a large soup pot, combine all ingredients, including reserved juice from tomatoes.

❖ Cover and bring to a boil over high heat. Reduce heat to low and simmer for 6 to 8 minutes, or until clams open. Do not overcook. Discard any clams that do not open. Place clams in a large bowl or individual bowls and serve with the savory tomato clam broth.

TARA'S TIP: Although the recipe call for only a ½ cup of wine I have found that it is much better with a full bottle. No, not to add to the pot, but to pour into a couple of glasses to enjoy with a few friends while this cooks!

Perfectly Poached Parchment Salmon

Don't be fooled! The fancy-looking meal in the picture opposite this page only looks like it was made in a restaurant. There's actually nothing to it! With just four ingredients, plus a little salt and pepper, you can whip up this quick, easy, and healthy meal any night of the week, any time of the year. You might even consider making this for your next date night!

Serves: 2   **Prep Time: 10 min**   **Cook Time: 15 min**

2 (12- x 14-inch) sheets of parchment paper

1 lemon, thinly sliced

16 stalks asparagus, trimmed to 6 inches

2 (4-ounce) salmon fillets

Salt for sprinkling

Black pepper for sprinkling

2 teaspoons olive oil

⁘ Preheat oven to 350 degrees F.

⁘ Fold each sheet of parchment in half crosswise; crease and unfold. Lay half the lemon slices on one half of each piece of parchment. Arrange 6 stalks of asparagus over lemon slices, then place a salmon fillet on top of asparagus. Place 2 more asparagus stalks on each piece of salmon. Sprinkle with salt and pepper and drizzle each with a teaspoon of oil.

⁘ Fold each piece of parchment over salmon and fold edges to seal. Place sealed packets on a rimmed 13- x 9-inch Lid-It or baking sheet.

⁘ Bake for 15 minutes. Remove from oven and carefully cut open parchment. (Be careful, the steam in each packet will be very hot.) Salmon should flake easily with a fork; if not, return to oven for a few minutes until fish flakes easily.

TARA'S TIP: The best way to seal the edges of the parchment paper is to make a series of folds and pleats around the edge, creating a crescent-shaped packet. The idea is to seal the edges so the fish steams as it cooks.

Homemade Shrimp Cakes

This is one of my go-to recipes whenever I'm in the mood for seafood. I love the versatility—these cakes are perfect on top of a salad or served alongside any combination of your favorite veggies. While you can definitely make these more traditional by using crab instead of the shrimp, I think there's something special about making them this way. You can really taste the shrimp in every bite!

Makes: 6   **Prep Time: 10 min**   **Cook Time: 10 min**

½ cup mayonnaise

1 egg

1 tablespoon Dijon mustard

2 cloves garlic, minced

1 tablespoon hot sauce

1 teaspoon seafood seasoning (I use Old Bay®.)

¼ teaspoon salt

¼ teaspoon black pepper

2 cups crushed buttery crackers

1 pound shrimp, peeled, deveined, and coarsely chopped

4 tablespoons olive oil

❖ In a large bowl, whisk together mayonnaise, egg, mustard, garlic, hot sauce, seafood seasoning, salt, and pepper. Gently stir in cracker crumbs and shrimp until just combined. Let mixture sit for 5 minutes before forming into 6 shrimp cakes.

❖ In a large skillet over medium heat, heat 2 tablespoons oil. Sauté shrimp cakes for 3 to 4 minutes per side or until the center is set and the outside is golden brown. Remove to a platter and cover with foil to keep warm. Repeat with remaining shrimp cakes, adding more oil as needed. Serve immediately or refrigerate until ready to use, then warm in a 300 degree oven for 10 minutes on a rimmed 13- x 9-inch Lit-It or baking sheet.

TARA'S TIP: Sometimes I serve these with my homemade tartar sauce (see note on page 150), other times I go with a classic cocktail sauce. Another favorite is a zesty Cilantro Lime Aioli. To make, just combine ½ cup mayonnaise, 1 tablespoon lime juice, and ¼ cup fresh cilantro in a blender until smooth.

Roadside Fish Fry

When I was a kid, my parents took us to visit my grandparents in Florida twice a year. Since we couldn't afford to fly, it always meant a long drive south. Because good seafood restaurants were hard to come by in New York, we made sure to check one out on every trip. It was always a treat to be able to order crispy, battered fish. Even today, I still think of this as a treat!.

Serves: 4 to 5   **Prep Time: 5 min**   **Cook Time: 20 min**

¾ cup all-purpose flour

2 tablespoons cornstarch

¼ teaspoon baking powder

¼ teaspoon baking soda

1 teaspoon sugar

½ teaspoon onion powder

½ teaspoon salt

¾ cup water

1 egg, beaten

Peanut oil for frying

2-½ pounds cod or haddock fillets, cut into individual portions

- In a large bowl, combine flour, cornstarch, baking powder, baking soda, sugar, onion powder, salt, water, and egg; mix well.

- In a large deep skillet over medium heat, heat 1 inch oil until hot, but not smoking. Dip fish into batter, coating completely, then fry for 4 to 5 minutes per side or until coating is golden and fish flakes easily with a fork. Drain on a paper towel-lined plate.

TARA'S TIP: I recommend frying this in peanut oil because of its high smoke point, which means your fish will fry better without burning. Since I'm basically a sauce queen, I always serve this with a homemade tartar sauce. To make it, just combine 1 cup mayonnaise, ¾ cup sweet pickle relish, ¼ cup finely chopped sweet onion, and the juice of ½ lemon. Stir it well and it's ready to serve. This makes about 2 cups, so if you have any left over, just store it in the fridge.

Asian-Style Tuna Steaks

I know a lot of people who like to order tuna steaks at restaurants, but shy away from making them at home because they feel it's too intimidating. I get it—it can be kind of daunting to cook tuna just right in a skillet. That's why I found a way to make it a little bit easier for everyone to enjoy this popular dish. My recipe is great for the home cook who wants great-tasting tuna that's quick and family-friendly.

Serves: 3 to 4   Prep Time: 10 min   Cook Time: 12 min   Chill Time: 60 min

4 tablespoons sesame oil, divided

1 tablespoon chopped garlic

½ teaspoon black pepper, divided

3 tablespoons soy sauce

1-¼ pounds sashimi grade tuna steaks

2 tablespoons sesame seeds

½ cup panko bread crumbs

1 teaspoon ground ginger

- In a large resealable plastic bag, mix 2 tablespoons sesame oil, the chopped garlic, ¼ teaspoon pepper, and the soy sauce. Add tuna steaks to bag, seal, and let marinate in refrigerator for 60 minutes.

- Meanwhile, in a small bowl, mix sesame seeds, bread crumbs, ginger, the remaining ½ teaspoon pepper and the remaining 2 tablespoons sesame oil.

- Preheat oven to 400 degrees F. Coat a rimmed 13- x 9-inch Lid-It or baking sheet with cooking spray. Remove tuna steaks from marinade, discard excess marinade, and place tuna steaks on Lid-It. Top evenly with sesame seed mixture and bake for 12 to 15 minutes for medium-rare or until desired doneness.

TARA'S TIP: If you like a nice sear on your tuna, throw it into a hot skillet for just a minute or so on each side. Then top with the sesame seed mixture and finish it off in the oven for about 10 to 12 minutes, depending on how you like it cooked.

My Grandkids' Favorite Mac & Cheese

My grandkids love mac and cheese—especially my mac and cheese. What they love most about it is seeing how high they can pull the cheese before it comes apart. (The mozzarella gives this one a really good stretch!) What adults love most about this is the trio of cheeses and the crunch of the cornflakes. Altogether, it makes for a creamy, dreamy dinner.

Serves: 6 to 8 **Prep Time: 20 min** **Cook Time: 35 min**

1 stick plus 2 tablespoons butter, divided

½ cup all-purpose flour

1 teaspoon salt

½ teaspoon black pepper

3-½ cups milk

8 ounces sharp cheddar cheese, shredded

8 ounces havarti cheese, shredded

1 pound large ridged elbow macaroni, cooked according to package directions

8 ounces mozzarella cheese, shredded

1-½ cups cornflakes

- Preheat oven to 375 degrees F. Coat a 13- x 9-inch baking dish with cooking spray.

- In a large pot over medium heat, melt 1 stick butter. Slowly stir in the flour, salt, and pepper; and cook until golden. Gradually whisk in milk, bring to a boil, and cook until thickened, stirring constantly.

- Reduce heat to medium-low. Add cheddar and havarti cheese and continue stirring until melted. Remove from heat, add macaroni, and mix until evenly coated. Stir in mozzarella cheese. Spoon mixture into baking dish.

- In a microwave-safe bowl, melt remaining 2 tablespoons butter in microwave. In a medium bowl, toss cornflakes with the butter. Sprinkle evenly over macaroni.

- Bake uncovered for 30 to 35 minutes or until top is golden and mixture is heated through.

TARA'S TIP: The large ribbed elbows don't just look pretty, they're practical too! I find that they do a better job of holding the cheese sauce. If for some reason you don't see these in your grocery store, my next go-to pasta for this would be shells, as they too hold lots of the sauce.

"Nudey" Gnocchi

Before you say, "But Tara, it's not 'Nudey,' it's gnudi!" I want you to know that I know. I just think it's such a cute name and a fun play on what is basically a lighter version of gnocchi. For those who don't know, both gnudi and gnocchi are types of Italian dumplings. But gnocchi is typically made with potato, where gnudi is all about the ricotta cheese. I hope you enjoy what I like to call my "Nudey" Gnocchi.

Serves: 5 to 6　　　　**Prep Time: 30 min**　　　　**Cook Time: 20 min**

1-½ pounds ricotta cheese

2-½ cups all-purpose flour

1 tablespoon plus
½ teaspoon salt, divided

1 stick butter

3 cloves garlic, minced

¼ teaspoon black pepper

1 tablespoon chopped
fresh parsley

Grated Parmesan cheese
for sprinkling

❖ In a large bowl, combine ricotta cheese and flour. Mix with your hands until dough is no longer sticky. On a lightly floured surface, roll a quarter of the dough into a ½-inch diameter tube-like rope. Cut into ½-inch pieces and gently twist each piece. Repeat with remaining dough.

❖ Fill a large pot with water, add 1 tablespoon salt, and bring to a boil over high heat. Gently drop 12 to 15 gnocchi at a time into boiling water. Gnocchi will rise to the top in 3 to 4 minutes. Cook for 1 more minute, then remove with a slotted spoon to a large bowl. Repeat with remaining gnocchi.

❖ Meanwhile, in a large skillet over low heat, melt butter. Add garlic, remaining ½ teaspoon salt, the pepper, parsley, and the gnocchi. Cook for 5 to 10 minutes or until heated through, stirring occasionally. Sprinkle with Parmesan cheese and serve.

TARA'S TIP: If you'd like to serve this with Vodka Sauce, simply do the following: In a medium saucepan over medium heat, combine 1 (24-ounce) jar spaghetti sauce and 1-¼ cups half-and-half and heat for 5 minutes. Stir in a ½ cup vodka, reduce heat to low, and continue to cook for 10 minutes or until sauce thickens, stirring occasionally.

Weeknight-Wonder Baked Rigatoni

The family is asking for lasagna, but you're feeling kind of tired after a long day. What do you do? I've got the answer for you right here! This rigatoni is so much like lasagna, you won't hear a single protest. It's a simple, hearty, pasta dish that delivers all the cheesy goodness a hungry family craves. In short, this rigatoni is bound to be one of your best weeknight wonders.

Serves: 6 to 8   **Prep Time: 5 min**   **Cook Time: 45 min**

1 pound rigatoni

1 (15-ounce) container ricotta cheese

3 cups (12 ounces) shredded mozzarella cheese, divided

1 teaspoon garlic powder

½ teaspoon salt

1 tablespoon slivered fresh basil

1 (24 ounce) jar spaghetti sauce

½ cup grated Parmesan cheese

⁘ Preheat oven to 350 degrees F. Coat a 13- x 9-inch baking dish or 3-quart casserole with cooking spray.

⁘ In a large pot of boiling salted water, cook rigatoni until just barely tender; drain and place in a large bowl. Add ricotta cheese, 1-½ cups mozzarella cheese, the garlic powder, salt, and basil; mix well.

⁘ Spread half the spaghetti sauce over bottom of baking dish. Spoon rigatoni mixture into baking dish; cover with remaining spaghetti sauce, then sprinkle with Parmesan cheese.

⁘ Bake for 30 minutes, then top with remaining 1-½ cups mozzarella cheese and bake for 10 more minutes or until heated through and the cheese is melted.

Just-the-Right-Size Lasagna Rollups

These meatless rollups are loaded with lots of cheese and veggies. They're super easy to make and reheat. In fact, I usually make a batch and once they're cooled, place them into plastic bags (two per bag), so that I can grab and reheat whenever I get a craving. The triple-cheesy goodness and the subtle sweetness of the carrots makes these hard to resist!

Makes: 14 rollups   **Prep Time: 20 min**   **Cook Time: 40 min**

1 (24-ounce) jar spaghetti sauce, divided

1 (32-ounce) container ricotta cheese

2 cups mozzarella cheese, divided

⅓ cup grated Parmesan cheese

1 (10-ounce) package frozen chopped spinach, thawed and squeezed dry

½ cup shredded carrot

2 eggs, beaten

1 teaspoon garlic powder

1 teaspoon salt

¼ teaspoon black pepper

14 lasagna noodles, cooked according to package directions

- Preheat oven to 375 degrees F. Pour half of the spaghetti sauce over bottom of a 13- x 9-inch baking dish.

- In a large bowl, combine ricotta cheese, 1 cup mozzarella cheese, the Parmesan cheese, spinach, carrot, eggs, garlic powder, salt, and pepper; mix until well blended.

- Spoon cheese mixture over lasagna noodles, spreading evenly with a knife, and roll up firmly. Place rollups on their end in prepared baking dish; top each with a spoonful of sauce. Cover tightly and bake for 30 to 35 minutes or until heated through

- Uncover, sprinkle with remaining mozzarella cheese and bake for 10 more minutes or until cheese is melted.

TARA'S TIP: Cooking these standing up makes the pasta a bit crispier. However, if you prefer your roll-ups a bit saucier, simply lay them down and proceed as suggested above.

Chopped Salad Pizza

I debated about where to place this recipe for a long while. Should it go with the other salads? Is it more of a pizza? By the end of my deliberation, I realized it didn't really matter. This is such a fun and tasty mash-up that I'll let you decide what to tell your family. (I find that calling it "pizza" works better in my house!)

Serves: 4 to 8 **Prep Time: 15 min** **Cook Time: 10 min**

1 tablespoon olive oil

2 cloves garlic, minced

1 (14-ounce) store-bought pizza crust

2 cups chopped romaine lettuce

½ cup cherry tomatoes, quartered

½ cucumber, peeled and diced

½ cup canned artichoke hearts, drained and cut into quarters

1 (4-ounce) can sliced black olives, drained

¼ cup roasted red pepper strips, drained

2 pepperoncini, sliced

⅓ cup vinaigrette dressing

- Preheat oven to 450 degrees F.

- In a small bowl, combine olive oil and garlic; mix well. Brush top of pizza crust with mixture and place directly on oven rack or on a pizza stone. Bake for 10 minutes or until crust is crisp.

- Meanwhile, in a large bowl, combine lettuce, tomatoes, cucumber, artichokes, olives, red peppers, and pepperoncini. Pour dressing over vegetables and toss until evenly coated.

- Top pizza crust with salad, cut into wedges, and serve.

TARA'S TIP: The combo of the hot crust with the chilled salad makes this salad even more desirable to me. It's like eating freshly baked rolls with a really good salad.

Deep Dish Pizza Bake

My version of a deep dish pizza is as easy as it gets. It's inspired by the many trips my family has made to Chicago. Every time we go, deep dish pizza is a must. Since everyone in my family has their own favorite toppings, I switch them up from time to time to be fair. Sometimes it's pepperoni, other times it's sausage crumbles or ham. One thing always holds true—this pizza is delicious!

Serves: 6 to 8   **Prep Time: 10 min**   **Cook Time: 25 min**

3 cups pancake and biscuit mix

1 cup plus 2 tablespoons water

1 (14-ounce) jar pizza sauce

½ (6-ounce) package sliced pepperoni

1-½ cups sliced fresh mushrooms

2 cups (8 ounces) shredded mozzarella cheese

:: Preheat oven to 375 degrees F. Coat a rectangular 3-quart baking dish with cooking spray.

:: In a medium bowl, stir biscuit mix and water until soft dough forms. Drop half of dough by spoonfuls evenly into bottom of baking dish. (Dough will not completely cover bottom of dish.)

:: Spoon 1 cup pizza sauce over dough. Arrange half the pepperoni slices and half the mushroom slices evenly over sauce. Top with 1 cup cheese. Repeat layers with remaining dough, pizza sauce, pepperoni, mushrooms, and cheese.

:: Bake for 25 to 30 minutes or until dough is cooked through and golden brown. Cut into squares and serve.

TARA'S TIP: If you prefer a thinner pizza crust, prepare this in a 13- x 9-inch baking pan and adjust your cooking time accordingly.

Italian Sausage 'n' Pepper Calzones

The traditional fair sandwich is loaded with lots of sausage, peppers, and onions. Naturally, it's one of my favorites. Because I believe that sausage and peppers make for a perfect marriage, I brought them together once again in this easy-peasy calzone recipe. While some things are meant to share, this one isn't one of them. Everyone gets their own!

Serves: 4   Prep Time: 20 min   Cook Time: 20 min

¾ pound bulk Italian sausage

1 onion, coarsely chopped

½ cup coarsely chopped bell pepper

3 cloves garlic, minced

½ cup spaghetti sauce

½ teaspoon dried Italian seasoning

1 (11-ounce) package refrigerated French bread dough

1 cup (4 ounces) shredded mozzarella cheese

Cooking spray

Grated Parmesan cheese

⁘ Preheat oven to 400 degrees F. Coat a 13- x 9-inch Lid-It or baking sheet with cooking spray.

⁘ In a large skillet over medium heat, cook sausage, onion, bell pepper, and garlic until sausage is broken up and no pink remains; drain well. Stir in spaghetti sauce and Italian seasoning.

⁘ Unroll bread dough onto a lightly floured cutting board. Using a rolling pin, roll out dough so it is about 16-inches square. Cut dough into 4 even squares and place them on a baking sheet.

⁘ Spoon equal amounts of the meat mixture onto center of each square and evenly top with mozzarella cheese. Fold the dough over the filling, creating a triangle. Press edges firmly together to seal. Repeat with remaining squares. Spray the top of each triangle with cooking spray, and sprinkle with Parmesan cheese.

⁘ Bake for 12 to 15 minutes or until the crust is golden and the filling is piping hot. Serve immediately.

TARA'S TIP: By now, you might have realized that I love dunking my food! That's why I always serve these with an extra side of warmed spaghetti sauce.

We're always thinking
OUTSIDE THE BOX
when it comes to design, and
INSIDE THE BOX
when it comes to
shipping each piece to you.

The Perfect Sides

Mouthwatering Melting Potatoes

O-M-G! I don't know if you've caught on to this already, but I love, love, love, buttery foods. When I discovered "melting potatoes," I was hooked. These potatoes are roasted with a delicious blend of butter and seasonings, then bathed in a flavor-packed, lemon-garlic sauce, before they're roasted again. There's so much flavor in every bite, they practically melt in your mouth (which must be why they're called melting potatoes!).

Serves: 6 to 8   **Prep Time: 10 min**   **Cook Time: 35 min**

½ stick butter, melted

1 teaspoon chopped fresh thyme

½ teaspoon salt

¼ teaspoon black pepper

2 pounds Yukon Gold potatoes, peeled and cut into ¾-inch-thick slices

¾ cup chicken broth

1 tablespoon lemon juice

2 cloves garlic, minced

- Preheat oven to 450 degrees F.

- In a large bowl, combine butter, thyme, salt, and pepper; mix well. Add potatoes and toss until evenly coated. Place potatoes in a single layer on a rimmed 13- x 9-inch Lid-It or baking sheet.

- Roast for 12 to 15 minutes per side or until golden brown, making sure to flip potatoes halfway through roasting.

- In a small bowl, combine broth, lemon juice, and garlic; mix well. Pour broth mixture over potatoes and roast for 10 more minutes or until potatoes are tender.

TARA'S TIP: I like using Yukon Gold potatoes in this recipe. They've got a slightly buttery flavor with moist flesh, which I think makes them doubly melt-worthy. However, you can make this with other potatoes, like russets.

My Favorite Sweet Potato Casserole

When it comes to adding marshmallows to your sweet potato casserole, you're either in or out. I'm all in! I love when a sweet potato casserole is just sweet enough, it can be mistaken for dessert. To make this, I use marshmallow crème (or fluff) instead of ordinary marshmallows. Unlike the marshmallows, the crème doesn't disappear when baked, so you get lots of marshmallow flavor in every bite.

Serves: 8 to 10

Prep Time: 15 min

Cook Time: 60 min

3 pounds sweet potatoes, peeled and cut into chunks

½ stick butter

½ teaspoon ground cinnamon

1-½ teaspoons salt

1 (7-½-ounce) jar marshmallow crème

¼ cup brown sugar

½ cup coarsely chopped pecans

- Preheat oven to 350 degrees F.

- Place cut sweet potatoes in a large pot with just enough water to cover. Bring to a boil over high heat and cook for 20 to 25 minutes or until fork tender; drain well.

- In a large bowl with an electric mixer, beat sweet potatoes, butter, cinnamon, and salt until smooth. Spoon half the potatoes into a 2-quart casserole dish. Spoon marshmallow crème evenly over sweet potatoes and top with remaining sweet potatoes.

- In a small bowl, combine brown sugar and pecans; mix well, then sprinkle evenly over potatoes.

- Bake for 40 to 45 minutes or until heated through and topping is golden.

TARA'S TIP: While I'm all about shortcuts, I think it's worth it to start with fresh sweet potatoes on this one. They make the casserole taste lighter and fresher.

Perfectly Creamy Cheesy Potatoes

This is a side dish that's easy enough to make during the week and special enough to serve when you've got company. I love that it can be comforting and elegant at the same time. Plus, each spoonful practically oozes with cheesy, creamy, goodness. As far as side dishes go, this one is a real crowd pleaser.

Serves: 4 to 6   **Prep Time: 15 min**   **Cook Time: 75 min**

1-½ cups shredded sharp cheddar cheese, divided

2 tablespoons all-purpose flour

1 cup milk

1 teaspoon onion powder

¾ teaspoon salt

¼ teaspoon black pepper

6 russet potatoes, cut into ¼-inch slices

3 tablespoons butter

2 tablespoons grated Parmesan cheese

Paprika for sprinkling

- Preheat oven to 375 degrees F. Coat an 8-inch square baking dish with cooking spray.

- In a medium bowl, combine 1 cup cheddar cheese, the flour, milk, onion powder, salt, and pepper.

- Arrange half the potato slices in baking dish. Pour half the cheese mixture over potatoes. Arrange remaining potatoes in baking dish, and pour remaining cheese mixture over potatoes. Dot with butter.

- Cover and bake for 45 minutes. Remove potatoes from oven, stir gently, cover, and return to oven for 20 more minutes. Uncover potatoes and sprinkle evenly with remaining ½ cup cheddar cheese and the Parmesan cheese. Sprinkle with paprika and return to oven to bake for 8 to 10 more minutes or until the potatoes are tender and the cheese is melted. Serve immediately.

TARA'S TIP: Go ahead and experiment with different cheeses! After you've tried it with cheddar, try Swiss or Monterey Jack. It's a good way to keep this recipe new and exciting for your family.

My Best Basic Mashed Potatoes

When I was a little girl, I used to complain about the lumps in the mashed potatoes. I would literally pick out the lumps and put them on the side of the plate. Then I would happily dig into the whipped part. It used to drive my mom nuts. While you won't find me picking out lumps these days, I still prefer my mashed potatoes smooth and creamy, with a big pat of butter on top!

Serves: 6 to 8   **Prep Time: 10 min**   **Cook Time: 25 min**

3 pounds russet potatoes, peeled and quartered

1 stick butter, softened

⅓ cup milk

½ teaspoon garlic powder

1 teaspoon salt

¼ teaspoon black pepper

Place potatoes in a large pot and fill with just enough water to cover. Cover and bring to a boil over high heat. Reduce heat to medium-low and cook for 20 minutes or until the potatoes are fork-tender; drain well.

Place potatoes in a large bowl and add remaining ingredients; beat with an electric mixer until smooth and creamy. (If you prefer your mashed potatoes chunky, just whip them less or stop by my mom's house, she still makes them that way.) Serve immediately.

TARA'S TIP: For those of you that like gravy on your mashed potatoes, I've got an easy recipe. All you do is place ½ stick butter in a saucepan. Once that's melted, whisk in ⅓ cup all-purpose flour and let that simmer until it's golden. Then slowly whisk in 2-½ cups beef broth, ¼ teaspoon salt, and ¼ teaspoon black pepper. After it's thickened, let it simmer until it's smooth, and pour it on!

Rancher's Picnic Potato Salad

When I was growing up, it was my job to peel the potatoes. While I loved helping out in the kitchen, I was not a fan of this job—it was so much work! Now as an adult, I often choose not to peel my potatoes in recipes like this potato salad. Not only does it give my recipes a more interesting look and taste, but I've learned that the skin is where most of the good stuff is!

Serves: 10 to 12   **Prep Time: 10 min**   **Cook Time: 20 min**

3 pounds red potatoes, unpeeled

1 cup mayonnaise

¾ cup sour cream

1 (1-ounce) packet dry ranch dressing mix

½ teaspoon black pepper

2 hard-boiled eggs, chopped

1 cup shredded cheddar cheese

4 slices cooked bacon, crumbled

1 stalk celery, sliced

2 scallions, thinly sliced

❖ Place potatoes in a soup pot with just enough water to cover; bring to a boil over high heat. Cook for 20 minutes or until fork-tender. Drain and let cool slightly. Cut potatoes into ½-inch chunks and place in a large bowl.

❖ Meanwhile, in a small bowl, combine mayonnaise, sour cream, ranch dressing mix, and pepper; mix well. Pour dressing over potatoes and mix gently. Add eggs, cheese, bacon, celery, and scallions, and toss until well combined. Serve or refrigerate until ready to serve.

TARA'S TIP: I like to mix in the mayo mixture with the potatoes while they're still warm. I find that the flavor seems to soak in better that way. Also, for a final finishing touch, I recommend garnishing your potato salad with a little extra bacon and scallions.

Apple Orchard Coleslaw

Coleslaw might just be the perfect side dish—it can be eaten year-round, there's no cooking involved, and it pairs perfectly with so many different foods. Plus it's easy to tweak and make your own. Aside from serving it next to my favorite foods, I also like using it as a topping on things like chicken breasts and burgers. It's a great alternative to your usual condiments and dressings!

Serves: 6 to 8　　　**Prep Time: 10 min**　　　**Chill Time: 60 min**

1 head cabbage, shredded (see Tip)

1 carrot, grated

1 apple, cored and diced

1 cup mayonnaise

3 tablespoons apple cider vinegar

1 teaspoon celery seed

1 teaspoon salt

½ teaspoon black pepper

1 tablespoon sugar (optional)

❖ In a large bowl, combine cabbage, carrot, and apple; set aside.

❖ In a small bowl, whisk mayonnaise, vinegar, celery seed, salt, pepper, and sugar, if desired. Pour mayonnaise mixture over coleslaw and toss until evenly coated. Cover and refrigerate for 60 minutes or until ready to serve.

TARA'S TIP: One head of cabbage yields about 8 cups of shredded cabbage. If you'd rather skip the cabbage prep, you can take a shortcut by buying prepared coleslaw mix. One to two bags should do it. Also, feel free to peel or not peel your apples. It's all about preference!

Gail's Perfect Sausage Stuffing

I've included a number of recipes from my mom, Gail, in this cookbook. (After all, she's the one who taught me how to cook!) But if there's one that truly represents her in every way, it's this one. Even though I've taken over with making this for the holidays, I still think she makes it the best (maybe she adds an extra dose of love?). From the flavors of the sage and sausage to the crunch of the celery, I love it all!

Serves: 8 to 10 **Prep Time: 15 min** **Cook Time: 60 min**

1 pound bulk Italian sausage

1 stick butter

2 celery stalks, chopped

1 large onion, chopped

1 (14-ounce) package stuffing cubes

½ (14-ounce) package herb-seasoned stuffing mix

1 egg, beaten

2 teaspoons ground sage

1 teaspoon thyme leaves

½ teaspoon salt

½ teaspoon black pepper

2 cups chicken broth

1 cup water

- Preheat oven to 350 degrees F.

- In a large skillet over medium-high heat, crumble and cook sausage for 5 to 7 minutes or until browned; drain liquid and set aside. In the same skillet over medium heat, melt butter. Add celery and onion and sauté for 6 to 8 minutes or until tender.

- In a large bowl, combine stuffing cubes, stuffing mix, cooked sausage, celery mixture, egg, sage, thyme, salt, and pepper. Add chicken broth and water; gently toss until thoroughly combined. Spoon stuffing into a 13- x 9-inch baking dish.

- Cover and bake for 30 minutes. Uncover and bake 20 more minutes or until it's heated through and the top is golden.

TARA'S TIP: Around the holidays when I know the oven will be filled to capacity, rather than baking this, I put it in a slow cooker. After 6 hours on LOW, it's done! Just dish it up in an autumn-themed baking dish and pass it around the table.

Skillet Quinoa Patties

My mom and I kind of stumbled on quinoa patties by mistake. We had some extra quinoa on hand, so she turned to me and said, "I think we can have fun with this." Of course, we totally did. Now, we make these all the time. Although they're slightly different each time, they always turn out really good. And for those of you who are carb-conscious, these are a better choice than traditional potato pancakes.

Makes: 12   **Prep Time: 20 min**   **Cook Time: 10 min**

1 cup quinoa, cooked according to package directions and cooled slightly

3 eggs, beaten

1 teaspoon salt

½ teaspoon black pepper

½ cup finely chopped onion

2 tablespoons finely chopped parsley

4 cloves garlic, minced

½ cup grated Parmesan cheese

1 cup dry bread crumbs

2 tablespoons olive oil

2 tablespoons butter

⁘ In a medium bowl, combine quinoa, eggs, salt, and pepper; mix well. Stir in onion, parsley, garlic, and Parmesan cheese. Add bread crumbs and mix gently. Form mixture into 12 (½-inch-thick) patties.

⁘ In a large skillet over medium heat, heat oil and butter until hot. Add patties, cover, and cook in batches for 5 to 6 minutes per side or until both sides are golden brown. Serve immediately or keep warm until ready to serve.

TARA'S TIP: These are great as-is, but if you want to make them even better, serve them with my Garlic Aioli. (See my tip on page 52.)

Farmhouse Green Beans

These green beans will add an extra side of comfort to your dinner plate. I've doctored them up with a little bit of bacon and some onion to make them even more flavorful. If you have people in your family who don't like eating their veggies, this is a good way to change their mind.

Serves: 6 to 8   **Prep Time: 10 min**   **Cook Time: 15 min**

1-½ pounds fresh green beans, trimmed

4 slices bacon, chopped

1 onion, cut into half-moon slices

½ cup white vinegar

⅓ cup sugar

❖ Place green beans in a soup pot and cover with water. Bring to a boil over high heat and cook for 4 to 5 minutes or until tender crisp; drain well and set aside.

❖ Meanwhile, in a large skillet over medium-high heat, cook bacon and onion for 5 to 7 minutes or until bacon is crisp, stirring often. Remove bacon and onion with a slotted spoon, reserving ¼ cup drippings in skillet. (Keep the rest of the bacon drippings in the fridge in a jar and use it for cooking if you'd like). Drain bacon and onion on paper towels and set aside.

❖ In a small bowl, combine vinegar and sugar. Pour mixture into skillet with drippings, and bring to a boil. Add green beans and cook over medium-high heat until heated through, stirring occasionally. Serve topped with bacon and onion mixture.

TARA'S TIP: If I'm pressed for time, I'll use frozen, thawed green beans instead. With frozen green beans, there's no need to trim or boil.

Bangin' Cauliflower

I know—no one uses the term "bangin'" anymore, but this is a play on one of my favorite shrimp appetizers from a certain restaurant whose name rhymes with "Conewish." (It's a shame you can't see me giggling right now!) I use cauliflower as a substitute quite a bit, so it was easy for me to come up with this idea. The cauliflower isn't just a healthier option; it also delivers great texture without sacrificing on flavor!

Serves: 10 to 12   **Prep Time: 10 min**   **Cook Time: 20 min**

1 egg

1 tablespoon water

1 cup Panko bread crumbs

1 tablespoon garlic powder

½ teaspoon onion powder

1 tablespoon chopped fresh parsley

1 (16-ounce) package frozen cauliflower florets, thawed

Cooking spray

Preheat oven to 400 degrees F. Lightly coat a rimmed 13- x 9-inch Lid-It or baking sheet with cooking spray.

In a small bowl, whisk egg and water. In another small bowl, combine bread crumbs, garlic powder, onion powder, and parsley; mix well.

Dip each cauliflower floret in egg mixture, then in bread crumb mixture. (Keep one hand for the dry ingredients and one for the wet; it will make things so much easier.) Place cauliflower on Lid-It and lightly coat with cooking spray.

Bake for 20 to 25 minutes or until golden and crispy.

TARA'S TIP: To enjoy the full bangin' experience, you've got to serve the cauliflower with my special dipping sauce. To make it, simply combine ¼ cup mayonnaise, 2 tablespoons sweet chili sauce, and 2 tablespoons hot sauce in a medium bowl. After giving it a stir, it's ready for drizzling or dipping.

Country Corn Casserole with Vanilla Butter

In the summer and fall, when fresh corn is easily available, you can bet you'll find me nibbling on an ear or two—maybe even roasting it on the grill. But in the wintertime, I turn to easy, creamy, corn casseroles, like this one. It delivers on classic tastes and warms me up from the inside out. To make it even sweeter, I top it with a homemade vanilla butter that's to-die-for.

Serves: 6 to 8   **Prep Time: 10 min**   **Cook Time: 50 min**

1 (8-½-ounce) package corn muffin mix

1 (15.25-ounce) can whole kernel corn, drained

1 (14.75-ounce) can cream-style corn

1 cup sour cream

¼ cup milk

2 eggs, beaten

3 tablespoons granulated sugar

¼ teaspoon salt

½ stick butter, melted

Vanilla Butter

3 tablespoons brown sugar

2 tablespoons butter, melted

2 teaspoons vanilla extract

❖ Preheat oven to 375 degrees F. Coat a 2-quart baking dish with cooking spray.

❖ In a large bowl, combine corn muffin mix, kernel corn, cream-style corn, sour cream, milk, eggs, granulated sugar, salt, and ½ stick butter; mix well. Pour mixture into baking dish.

❖ To make the Vanilla Butter, in a small bowl, combine all topping ingredients; spoon over corn mixture.

❖ Bake for 50 to 55 minutes or until set in center and the top is golden.

Holiday-Special Cranberry Sauce

The holidays just aren't the holidays without homemade cranberry sauce—at least not in my house! My mom, Gail, has been making cranberry sauce from scratch, for as long as I can remember. She taught me that when it comes to cranberry sauce, homemade is always the way to go. Sure I've bought the canned stuff in the past (sometimes, you just find yourself in a pinch!), but never during the holidays!

Makes: 2 Cups　　　**Prep Time: 5 min**　　　**Cook Time: 10 min**

1 (12-ounce) package fresh cranberries

1 cup sugar

1 tablespoon fresh orange or lemon zest

¼ teaspoon allspice

¼ cup water

⅛ teaspoon salt

In a medium saucepan over medium-high heat, combine all ingredients. Bring to a boil, then reduce heat to low and simmer for 10 to 15 minutes or until cranberries burst and mixture starts to thicken. Let cool slightly, then transfer to a serving bowl.

Serve warm or allow to completely, then cover and chill until ready to serve.

TARA'S TIP: This cranberry sauce is more tart than sweet. If once you've tasted it, you want to sweeten it up a bit, just add an additional ¼ cup sugar and cook it a few more minutes (so the sugar dissolves).

All-American Baked Beans

Baked beans are a summertime staple. If I'm having a backyard barbecue, you can bet I'm making these. Mine are made from scratch and feature the perfect amount of sweetness (you should know I like things on the sweeter side!). I'm also a big believer that baked beans should always be made with bacon and onion, since they add great flavor and texture.

Serves: 6 to 8   Prep Time: 10 min   Cook Time: 55 min

1-¼ cups ketchup

½ cup water

3 tablespoons molasses

1 tablespoon Worcestershire sauce

½ cup brown sugar

½ teaspoon dry mustard

½ teaspoon salt

3 (15.5-ounce) cans navy beans, drained

6 slices uncooked bacon, chopped (see Tip)

½ cup diced onion

- Preheat oven to 350 degrees F.

- In a large bowl, combine ketchup, water, molasses, Worcestershire sauce, brown sugar, dry mustard, and salt; mix well. Add navy beans, bacon, and onion, and mix until thoroughly combined.

- Spoon mixture into 4 (9-ounce) ramekins or a 1-½-quart baking dish. Bake for 55 to 60 minutes or until bubbly hot and the sauce thickens slightly.

TARA'S TIP: I like to chop the bacon into larger pieces, since the pieces will cook down during baking. Also, if you're making these for a special holiday get-together, why not break out the seasonal bakeware? My Red, White, & Blue collection (pictured) is perfect for a 4th of July cookout!

Garlic Parmesan Twisters

I've never met a carb I didn't like, so when it comes to setting out a bread basket at the dinner table—I'm all in. While dinner rolls are delicious and breadsticks are pretty darn good too, I prefer to make something with a special twist (pun intended!). These twisted sticks pair well with anything and everything—not just your spaghetti dinner!

Makes: 16 **Prep Time: 10 min** **Cook Time: 20 min**

1 (17.3-ounce) package frozen puff pastry sheets, thawed

½ stick butter, melted and divided

1 teaspoon garlic powder

½ teaspoon salt

2 tablespoons grated Parmesan cheese

1 tablespoon chopped fresh parsley

2 teaspoons sesame seeds

❖ Preheat oven to 375 degrees F. On a cutting board, unfold both sheets of puff pastry.

❖ In a small bowl, combine 2 tablespoons butter, the garlic powder, and salt; mix well, then brush over 1 pastry sheet. Sprinkle evenly with Parmesan cheese and parsley. Place second sheet of puff pastry on top of the cheese and press down lightly. Cut lengthwise into ½-inch-wide strips and gently twist each strip, as shown in the photo.

❖ Place breadsticks on 13- x 9-inch Lid-Its or baking sheets. Brush with remaining 2 tablespoons butter and sprinkle with sesame seeds.

❖ Bake for 20 to 25 minutes or until golden. Let cool slightly and serve warm or at room temperature.

TARA'S TIP: These can be made ahead of time and stored in an airtight, Lock & Lock® container. When ready to serve, just place them on a baking sheet in a 300-degree oven for about 10 minutes or until they are nice and crispy.

The key to our design
is that every piece
must be

multi-functional,

from practical
to whimsical.

Sweet Tooth Sensations

Crazy Good Chocolate Cake

Who doesn't love a good chocolate cake? Not anyone I know! In my family, chocolate cake is always welcomed with open arms. To make things easy, I doctor a box of devil's food cake mix with a little sour cream. Then, I finish it off with a from-scratch chocolate frosting. This cake is so rich and moist, I recommend serving it with shot glasses of milk!

Serves: 12 to 16   Prep Time: 10 min   Cook Time: 30 min

1 package devil's food cake mix

½ cup sour cream

½ cup vegetable oil

3 eggs

1 cup water

Fudgy Chocolate Frosting

2 sticks butter, softened

1 cup unsweetened cocoa powder

2 teaspoons vanilla extract

5 cups powdered sugar

⅓ cup milk

- Preheat oven to 350 degrees F. Coat two 8-inch round cake pans with cooking spray.

- In a large bowl, with an electric mixer, beat cake mix, sour cream, oil, eggs, and water until well combined. Divide batter evenly between cake pans.

- Bake for 30 to 35 minutes or until a toothpick inserted in center comes out clean. Allow to cool slightly, then remove to a wire rack to cool completely.

- Meanwhile, to make the Fudgy Chocolate Frosting, in a large bowl with an electric mixer on low speed, beat butter and cocoa until thoroughly mixed. Slowly add the remaining ingredients and mix until smooth. (If you do this too quickly you'll have a cloud of powdered sugar all over your kitchen.)

- Place one cake layer on a cake plate; spread top with frosting. Place second layer over first and frost top and sides with remaining frosting. Serve immediately or chill until ready to serve.

TARA'S TIP: Give your cake an old-fashioned look by adding swirls to the frosting. You can do this with the back of a soup spoon. Just have fun and before you know it you'll be a pro!

Perfect Pineapple Upside-Down Cake

This traditional dessert combines two of my favorites: pineapples (my favorite fruit) and vanilla cake. It's a dessert that I've watched my grandmother and mother make, and that I'm proud to pass along to the next generation. Another fun thing I love about it is how the pineapple rings make it easy to figure out individual portions (one pineapple ring piece is one portion). It's yummy, easy, and organized—I love it!

Serves: 12   **Prep Time: 10 min**   **Cook Time: 30 min**

¾ cup packed light brown sugar

1 stick butter, melted

1 (20-ounce) can pineapple slices, drained

1 (8-ounce) can pineapple slices, drained

12 maraschino cherries

1 package yellow cake mix

1 cup water

¼ cup vegetable oil

3 eggs

∷ Preheat oven to 350 degrees F.

∷ Sprinkle brown sugar evenly over bottom of a 13- x 9-inch baking dish. Pour butter evenly over brown sugar. In a single layer, arrange pineapple slices (from both cans) over butter and place a cherry in center of each slice.

∷ In a large bowl with an electric mixer, beat cake mix, water, oil, and eggs until well combined. Pour batter evenly over pineapple layer. Bake for 30 to 35 minutes or until a toothpick inserted in center comes out clean. Let the cake cool for about 10 minutes. (Set a timer because if it cools too much, it will stick when you try flipping it.)

∷ Run a knife around the edge of the pan to loosen it. Place a 13- x 9-inch Lid-It on top of the pan and carefully flip the pan over. Serve warm or cooled completely.

TARA'S TIP: If you don't have a 13-x 9-inch Lid-It to flip this over on, a cutting board will do the trick.

Glazed Pumpkin Ring Cake

When temperatures start dropping and leaves begin changing their colors, it's time to get back to baking fall favorites. One of the ways that I make the transition into fall is with this pumpkin spice cake. And since I think everything is better with a little chocolate, I load mine up with plenty of mini chocolate chips. If you needed another reason to love the fall, you've got one here.

Serves: 10 to 12 **Prep Time: 10 min** **Cook Time: 40 min**

1 package spice cake mix

1 (15-ounce) can pure pumpkin (not pie filling)

3 eggs

¾ cup water

½ cup mini chocolate chips

1-¼ cups powdered sugar

1 teaspoon vanilla extract

2 tablespoons milk

⁖ Preheat oven to 350 degrees F. Coat a fluted tube pan with cooking spray.

⁖ In a large bowl with an electric mixer, beat cake mix, pumpkin, eggs, and water until well mixed; stir in chocolate chips. (I suggest tossing the chocolate chips with a tablespoon of powdered sugar before adding them to the batter. It helps suspend them evenly in the batter while the cake bakes). Pour into pan.

⁖ Bake for 40 to 45 minutes or until a toothpick comes out clean. Cool cake for about 15 minutes, then invert it onto a wire rack to cool completely.

⁖ Meanwhile, in a medium bowl, whisk powdered sugar, vanilla, and milk together until smooth. When the cake is cool, place it on a cake platter and spoon the glaze over it. (I like the look when the glaze sort of puddles onto the serving platter.)

Fudge-Filled Chocolate Mint Cupcakes

A while ago, I came across a quote that made me smile; it said, "Cupcakes are muffins that believed in miracles." Well guys, this is a chocolate mint miracle. For everyone who loves the combo of chocolate and mint, these are just for you. They're fun to make and even more fun to eat. Plus depending on whether you serve them right out of the fridge or at room temperature, determines how ooey-gooey your chocolatey centers will be.

Makes: 20 Cupcakes   **Prep Time: 20 min**   **Cook Time: 20 min**

1 package chocolate fudge cake mix, batter prepared according to package directions

1-½ cups semisweet chocolate chips

⅓ cup heavy cream

Mint Buttercream

2 sticks butter, softened

3 teaspoons mint extract

6 cups powdered sugar

¼ cup milk

10 crème de menthe chocolate mint candies, cut in half (I use Andes®.)

⁘ Preheat oven to 350 degrees F. Line 20 muffin cups with paper liners. Spoon batter into muffin cups, filling each about ¾ full. Bake for 18 to 22 minutes or until a toothpick comes out clean. Let cool completely.

⁘ Using an apple corer or paring knife, cut a hole in center of each cupcake ¾ of the way down. (Make sure you don't cut all the way through to the bottom.) Remove cut centers.

⁘ In a medium microwave-safe bowl, combine the chocolate chips and heavy cream. Microwave for 60 to 90 seconds or until mixture is smooth, stirring occasionally. (I suggest microwaving for 30 seconds at a time, then stirring and repeating until chocolate is melted and smooth.) Let cool slightly. Place mixture into a plastic storage bag, snip off corner, and fill cupcake centers.

⁘ To make the Mint Buttercream, in a large bowl with an electric mixer, beat butter and mint extract until creamy. Gradually add the powdered sugar and milk, and mix until fluffy and smooth.

⁘ Frost or pipe the cupcakes as shown, then garnish each with a piece of chocolate mint candy. Serve or refrigerate until ready to serve.

No-Bake S'mores Cake

There's no campfire needed to make this sweet and tasty treat! Since s'mores are one of my favorite treats (seriously, I make them all the time), I came up with another great way to enjoy the flavor trio all year-round. This no-bake cake has the chocolate, the marshmallows, and the graham crackers, but doesn't require any baking, roasting, or melting. It makes me so happy!

Serves: 10 to 12   **Prep Time: 10 min**   **Chill Time: 4 hrs**

1 (14.4-ounce) box graham crackers

2 (4-serving-size) packages chocolate fudge instant pudding mix

3 cups milk

2-¼ cups mini-marshmallows, divided

1 (8-ounce) container frozen whipped topping, thawed

1 (1.55-ounce) chocolate bar

⁂ Line the bottom of an ungreased 13- x 9-inch baking dish with one-third of the graham crackers. (Arrange them so they cover the bottom completely.)

⁂ In a large bowl, whisk together pudding mix and milk, stirring until mixture thickens. Fold in 2 cups of marshmallows.

⁂ Spread half of pudding mixture over graham crackers in baking dish. Place another layer of graham crackers over the pudding, and repeat one more time until all the pudding and most of the graham crackers are used up. (You may have a few graham crackers left over; I like to nibble on them while this is firming up.)

⁂ Slather whipped topping over the top. With a vegetable peeler, "peel" chocolate bar over whipped topping, creating chocolate curls. Sprinkle with remaining marshmallows. Cover and chill for 4 to 6 hours or until it's firm enough to cut into squares.

TARA'S TIP: Want to freeze a few for later? Go ahead and do it! I like to freeze individual portions so I can grab-and-go when the cravings set in.

Candy Bar Brownie Bombe

I bet you never thought you could do something like this at home! I've had friends tell me that this dessert looks like something they'd order at a restaurant, but not something they would ever try at home. I never understood why, so I challenged them with this recipe. Turns out, everyone can do it. So now, it's your turn! I promise you, it's easy and the rewards are sweet.

Serves: 10 to 12   Prep Time: 10 min   Cook Time: 20 min   Chill Time: 6 hrs

1 package brownie mix, batter prepared according to package directions

1 quart vanilla ice cream, softened

1-¼ cups chopped assorted candy bars, divided

1 (8-ounce) container frozen whipped topping, thawed

- Preheat oven to 350 degrees F. Bake brownies according to package directions for a 13- x 9-inch baking dish; let cool. (Follow the directions for fudgy brownies, rather than cake-like ones.)

- Line a 2-quart bowl with plastic wrap. Cut brownies into squares and line bowl with about ⅔ of brownies, pressing them together until the inside of the bowl is completely lined, up to 1-inch from the top.

- In a medium bowl, gently mix the softened ice cream with ¾ cup of the chopped candy bars. Spoon ice cream mixture into brownie bowl, pressing it firmly, so it's well-packed. Place remaining brownies over top and press firmly into ice cream. Cover with plastic wrap and freeze for at least 6 hours or until ice cream is frozen solid.

- Remove plastic wrap from top of bowl. Turn the bowl over onto a large serving platter. Remove bowl, then remove remaining plastic wrap. (You may need to be patient until the bowl warms up enough for the brownie bowl to come out.) Frost with whipped topping; sprinkle with remaining ½ cup chopped candy. Keep frozen until ready to serve.

Cupid's Spoon Cheesecake

This is the ultimate, no-stress cheesecake. You don't need a springform pan and you don't have to worry about it cracking or slumping. There's not even any baking! Instead, you'll get to enjoy a light and fluffy, no-bake, no-crust cheesecake that delivers all the classic flavor you love. Oh yeah, and when it comes time to serve it, you'll only need a spoon.

Serves: 6 to 8   **Prep Time: 5 min**   **Chill Time: 3 hrs**

1 (8-ounce) package cream cheese, softened

½ cup sugar

1 cup (½ pint) sour cream

2 teaspoons vanilla extract

1 (8-ounce) container frozen whipped topping, thawed

¼ cup graham cracker crumbs

1 cup fresh raspberries for garnish

- In a large bowl with an electric mixer, beat cream cheese until smooth. Gradually beat in sugar, then blend in sour cream and vanilla. Fold in whipped topping until well mixed.

- Spoon mixture into a 1-½-quart baking dish. Chill for 3 to 4 hours or until set.

- Decorate with graham cracker crumbs around the edge and fresh raspberries, as desired.

TARA'S TIP: Be sure to make this in any of your temp-tations seasonal favorites. One year, I served it as a sweet treat on Valentine's Day (like in the photo). You can even divide the mixture into individual ramekins, so everyone gets their own. By the way, if you'd like to lighten up your cheesecake, go ahead and use reduced fat cream cheese and sour cream. It'll still taste great, but with less fat and calories.

Black & White Cookie Cheesecake

This traditional cheesecake is made with my go-to, store-bought cookies. (I'll give you a hint, they start with an "O" and end with an "O".) There are cookies in the crust, in the filling, and on top. The nice thing about this cheesecake is that you can change it up every time by using a different flavored cookie. As you know, my go-to cookie is available in different flavors every season, so it's easy to be adventurous!

Serves: 12   Prep Time: 20 min   Cook Time: 60 min   Chill Time: 8 hrs

1 (20-ounce) package cream-filled chocolate sandwich cookies, divided

¾ stick butter, melted

3 (8-ounce) packages cream cheese, softened

1-¼ cups sugar, divided

4 eggs

2 teaspoons vanilla extract, divided

1 (16-ounce) container sour cream

1 tablespoon unsweetened cocoa powder

Whipped cream for garnish

Preheat oven to 350 degrees F. Place 30 cookies in a plastic storage bag and crush them with a rolling pin or a meat mallet. (Make sure you close the bag first before crushing them or you'll have one heck of a mess on your hands.) Place crumbs in a medium bowl with the butter; mix well, then spread mixture into bottom and halfway up sides of a 10-inch springform pan. Chill until ready to use.

In a large bowl with an electric mixer on medium speed, beat cream cheese and 1 cup sugar until creamy. Add the eggs, one at a time, beating well after each addition, then add 1 teaspoon vanilla and mix well. Set aside 6 cookies for garnish, then break up remaining cookies. Stir cookie pieces into cream cheese mixture, then pour into crust.

Bake for 55 to 60 minutes or until firm. Remove from oven and let cool for 5 minutes.

Meanwhile, in a medium bowl, using a spoon, stir together sour cream, cocoa, remaining ¼ cup sugar, and remaining 1 teaspoon vanilla until well combined. Carefully spread sour cream mixture over top of cheesecake then bake for 5 more minutes.

Let cool, then chill for 8 hours or overnight. Cover until ready to serve. When ready to serve, remove from pan to a serving plate. Score the cake into 12 pieces and dollop each with whipped cream. Cut the 6 reserved cookies in half and place half a cookie on each dollop of whipped cream. Refrigerate until ready to serve.

Red Velvet Poke Cake

Red velvet cakes are people pleasers. Seriously, people go crazy over them! While I love making them from scratch, sometimes I take a shortcut by starting with a boxed cake mix. And when you take it to the next level by "poking it," all the better. I fill the holes with a vanilla cream and top it with a traditional, homemade, cream cheese frosting and finish it off with red sprinkles. It disappears every time!

Serves: 12 to 15   Prep Time: 15 min   Cook Time: 25 min   Chill Time: 4 hrs

1 package red velvet cake mix, batter prepared according to package directions

1 (4-serving-size) package instant white chocolate pudding and pie filling mix

2 cups milk

Cream Cheese Frosting

1 (8-ounce) package cream cheese, softened

1 stick butter, softened

1 (16-ounce) package powdered sugar

1 teaspoon vanilla extract

Red nonpareil sprinkles for sprinkling (optional)

Preheat oven to 350 degrees F. Coat a 13- x 9-inch baking dish with cooking spray. Add batter and bake according to package directions; let cool.

Using the handle of a wooden spoon or an apple corer, poke holes about 1-inch apart all over top of cake.

In a large bowl, whisk pudding mix and milk until slightly thickened. Pour mixture onto top of cake and spread so that it fills the holes.

To make Cream Cheese Frosting, in a medium bowl with an electric mixer, beat cream cheese, butter, powdered sugar, and vanilla until smooth.

Spread frosting over pudding, cover, and refrigerate at least 4 hours or until ready to serve. Garnish with nonpareils, if desired.

TARA'S TIP: Make sure the holes are big enough to hold the creamy pudding, but not too big that it takes away from the richness of the cake.

Cranberry Bog Custard Pie

Have you ever visited a cranberry bog? If you have, then you've seen how the berries float on the water. This pie sort of does something similar. Although you put the cranberries at the bottom and pour the custard filling on top, during the baking process, the cranberries actually rise to the top—just like they do in bogs! This quick and easy dessert is sure to impress your friends and family.

Serves: 8 to 10   Prep Time: 5 min   Cook Time: 55 min   Chill Time: 2 hrs

1 refrigerated rolled pie crust (from a 14.1-ounce package)

1 (12-ounce) package fresh cranberries (see Tip)

1-½ cups sugar

⅓ cup all-purpose flour

½ teaspoon salt

1 cup heavy cream

3 eggs, beaten

2 tablespoons butter, melted

1 teaspoon vanilla extract

Preheat oven to 350 degrees F. Unroll pie crust and press into pie dish; flute edges. Place cranberries in crust.

In a large bowl, whisk sugar, flour, and salt. Add heavy cream, eggs, butter, and vanilla, and whisk until thoroughly combined. Pour mixture evenly over cranberries.

Bake for 55 to 60 minutes or until custard is set in center. Let cool, then refrigerate for at least 2 hours or until ready to serve.

TARA'S TIP: If you're craving this outside of cranberry season, you can use frozen cranberries instead. Just make sure they're slightly thawed before placing them in the crust.

Peanut Butter Cup Pie

Just like the story of Goldilocks and the three bears, it took a few tries before I got this pie "just right." Lucky for you, you get to reap the rewards! This pie is a peanut butter and chocolate lover's dream, with a creamy consistency and a chocolate cookie crust. It's a good pie to make any day of the year, as it always makes people smile.

Serves: 8 to 10   Prep Time: 10 min   Cook Time: 8 min   Chill Time: 8 hrs

1-¾ cups finely crushed chocolate wafer cookies

¼ cup granulated sugar

¾ stick butter, melted

1 cup creamy peanut butter

1 (8-ounce) package cream cheese, softened

1-½ cups powdered sugar

1 teaspoon vanilla extract

1 (12-ounce) container frozen whipped topping, thawed, divided

1 cup chopped peanut butter cups, divided

Preheat oven to 350 degrees F. In a medium bowl, combine cookie crumbs, granulated sugar, and butter; mix well. Press crumbs into the bottom and up sides of a 9-inch deep dish pie dish. Bake for 8 minutes, then let cool completely.

In a large bowl with an electric mixer on medium speed, beat peanut butter and cream cheese until smooth. Beat in powdered sugar and vanilla until smooth. Fold in (do not beat) 3 cups whipped topping and ¾ cup chopped peanut butter cups. Spoon mixture into crust.

Dollop with remaining whipped topping and peanut butter cups. Chill for 8 hours or overnight; serve

TARA'S TIP: In some recipes, it's okay to use a lower fat or reduced sugar whipped topping instead of a regular one, but I wouldn't suggest it for this recipe. In all my trials, I found that the regular whipped topping seemed to hold this pie together a bit better.

Cinnamon Apple Cobbler

You may have heard me mention one or two times on-air, that one of the big reasons why I created temp-tations was for ooey-gooey desserts, like this one. I wanted a cooking vessel that would be non-stick enough to bake and serve my gooiest desserts, without having to pay the price at the kitchen sink later on. Anyway, here's a dessert that's all-American and all-delicious. Go on and dig in!

Serves: 8 to 10 **Prep Time: 15 min** **Cook Time: 45 min**

2 cups sugar, divided

1-¾ cups all-purpose flour, divided

¾ teaspoon ground cinnamon, divided

6 large tart apples, peeled, cored, and cut into ¼-inch-thick slices

1-½ teaspoons baking powder

½ teaspoon salt

2 eggs, beaten

1 stick butter, melted

Vanilla ice cream

- Preheat oven to 350 degrees F.

- In a large bowl, combine ¾ cup sugar, ¼ cup flour, and ½ teaspoon cinnamon; mix well. Add apples and toss until evenly coated. Place apples in a 2-quart baking dish and set aside.

- In a medium bowl, combine remaining 1-½ cups flour, remaining 1-¼ cups sugar, remaining ¼ teaspoon cinnamon, the baking powder, and salt; mix well. Add eggs and mix until crumbly. Sprinkle topping mixture evenly over apples and drizzle with butter.

- Bake for 45 to 50 minutes or until the topping is golden and the apple mixture is bubbling hot. Serve warm with vanilla ice cream.

TARA'S TIP: If you're running short on apples, but find yourself with a few pears on hand, go ahead and mix the two. You can use three of each to make a "pearfectly" good cobbler. Sorry, I couldn't resist.

Bumbleberry Shortcake Parfaits

Angel food cake is my favorite. In fact, every year on my birthday, my mom bakes me one from scratch. It's so good, I've found other ways to incorporate it into my desserts. Here, I've teamed it with what's called a bumbleberry sauce (which is just a fancy way to say a mixed berry sauce), and topped it off with fresh whipped cream. Ah, if only everything in life was this good and this easy!

Makes: 8

1 cup fresh strawberries, sliced in half

1 cup fresh raspberries

1 cup fresh blueberries

1 cup fresh blackberries

½ cup granulated sugar

2 tablespoons raspberry liqueur (optional)

1 cup heavy cream

¼ cup powdered sugar

1 (10-inch) store-bought angel food cake, cut into cubes

Prep Time: 1 hr

In a large bowl, combine strawberries, raspberries, blueberries, and blackberries; sprinkle with granulated sugar and liqueur, if desired. Mix well and let sit for 45 to 60 minutes or until sugar dissolves into a syrup, stirring occasionally.

Meanwhile, in a medium bowl with an electric mixer, beat heavy cream and powdered sugar until stiff peaks form; refrigerate until ready to serve.

Place cake cubes in parfait glasses or into a large serving bowl (if you want to make one big version of this). Spoon berries with their juice over cake and dollop with whipped cream. Serve immediately.

TARA'S TIP: Mint makes the perfect garnish for this dessert. If the mint you've brought home from the grocery store looks like it's had better days, bring it back to life by placing it in a large, plastic storage container with a tablespoon or two of water. Give it a shake, place it in the fridge, and the next day it will look like it was just picked.

Hodge Podge Cookies

Do you have a hard time choosing between a crispy cookie and a chewy one? Do you like the combination of sweet and salty? Do you want it all? You got it! These cookies are all of the above and more. In fact, you might say they've got everything but the kitchen sink. Go ahead and create your own hodge podge of mix-ins. Maybe add in your favorite candies, nuts, chips ... you name it.

Makes: About 36   **Prep Time: 15 min**   **Cook Time: 10 min**

½ cup rolled oats

2 cups all-purpose flour

1 teaspoon baking soda

½ teaspoon salt

1 stick butter, softened

¾ cup packed brown sugar

¾ cup granulated sugar

1 teaspoon vanilla extract

2 eggs

1-½ cups assorted chopped candy bars

1 cup coarsely chopped pretzels

Preheat oven to 350 degrees F. In a food processor or blender, pulse oats until fine. In a large bowl, combine oats, flour, baking soda, and salt; mix well.

In another large bowl with an electric mixer on medium speed, cream together butter, the two sugars, and vanilla. Add eggs and mix until smooth. Stir in oats mixture; mix well.

Stir candy and pretzels into dough; mix well. Drop dough by heaping teaspoonfuls onto 13- x 9-inch Lid-Its or baking sheets about 1-inch apart.

Bake for 10 to 12 minutes or until cookies are light brown around edges. Let cool for 5 minutes, then remove to wire racks to cool completely.

TARA'S TIP: If you want to get a head start, make the dough a day or two in advance and keep it in the fridge. When you're ready to make them, just stir in your add-ins (candies, pretzels, chips) before baking.

Old World Sugar Cookies

Some people think "Old World" means you have to do a lot of work, but I think it's more about getting those classic flavors right. And when you have the perfect cookie, you want to make sure it looks extra special. And what is more special than my Old World design, especially when you create it out of gum drops and candy-coated chocolate?

Makes: About 2 dozen (see Tip)   Prep Time: 15 min   Cook Time: 8 min

2 sticks salted butter, softened

1-½ cups powdered sugar

3 teaspoons vanilla extract

1 egg

3-½ cups all-purpose flour, plus extra for rolling

1 (16-ounce) container white frosting

Gum drops

Mini candy-coated chocolate candies

Preheat oven to 400 degrees F. In a large bowl with an electric mixer on low speed, mix butter, powdered sugar, and vanilla just until combined. Increase the speed to medium, and cream the mixture until light and fluffy. Add the egg and continue to beat. Add flour all at once and mix on low speed until combined and dough begins to pull away from bowl.

Dust work surface with flour. Cut dough in half, setting one half aside. With a rolling pin, roll out remaining half of dough to ¼-inch-thickness, flouring generously so that it doesn't stick to the rolling pin or counter.

Using a 2-½- to 3-inch round cookie or biscuit cutter, cut out dough and place on 13- x 9-inch Lid-Its or baking sheets, about 1-inch apart. Repeat with remaining dough. (Make sure you re-roll the "scraps" of dough so you don't waste any.)

Bake for 8 to 10 minutes or until cookies are set. (Do not allow cookies to brown.) Cool on Lid-Its, then frost. Serve as-is or if you want to decorate them to look like my Old World pattern, start by placing a gum drop on a cutting board dusted with granulated sugar. After rolling it out with a rolling pin, use a paring knife to cut out the leaf shapes of the pattern. (Use any color gum drops.) For the center, use red or yellow mini candy-coated chocolate candies.

TARA'S TIP: The amount of cookies you'll end up with will depend on the size of your cookie cutter. We used a 2-inch round cutter and got about 2 dozen.

Mom's Crispy Cinnamon Cookies

These cinnamon-spiced cookies are the perfect little pick-me-up that I learned from my mom. They're great for snacking on whenever and wherever, and if you keep them stored in an airtight container ... they'll last you pretty much forever. I love that they're flaky and flavorful, so you get satisfied with just one (although I bet you can't stop at one!). With just 4 ingredients, these are some of the easiest cookies I make.

Makes: 40   Prep Time: 10 min   Cook Time: 12 min   Chill Time: 60 min

⅓ cup brown sugar

1 teaspoon ground cinnamon

1 (14.1-ounce) package refrigerated rolled pie crust (2 crusts)

½ stick butter, melted

In a small bowl, combine brown sugar and cinnamon; mix well and set aside.

On a flat surface with a rolling pin, roll out 1 pie crust until it's about ⅛-inch thick. Brush with half of the melted butter, then sprinkle with half of the sugar-cinnamon mixture. Roll up and wrap tightly in plastic wrap. Repeat with remaining dough, butter, and sugar-cinnamon mixture. Refrigerate for at least 1 hour.

When ready to bake, preheat oven to 375 degrees F. Unwrap dough, and place rolls on a cutting board. Trim off ends, and discard. Cut each log into 20 slices. Place slices on 13- x 9-inch Lid-Its or baking sheets.

Bake for 12 to 14 minutes or until bottoms are crispy. Serve warm or when cooled, store in an airtight container.

Pecan Turtle Crispy Treats

I'll give you a minute to really take in everything you're looking at in the photo opposite this page. Yes, this is a childhood favorite and yes, I've made it even better. Not only do you get all that crispy marshmallow-y goodness, but now you also get chocolate ... and buttery pecans ... and ooey-gooey caramel. These are just unbelievably good and definitely worth sharing with everyone you care about.

Makes: 24   Prep Time: 15 min   Cook Time: 10 min   Chill Time: 30 min

½ stick butter

1 (10-ounce) package marshmallows

7 cups crispy rice cereal

20 caramel candies

2 tablespoons heavy cream

24 pecan halves

1 cup semisweet chocolate chips

1 teaspoon vegetable shortening

⁘ Coat a rimmed 13- x 9-inch Lid-It or baking dish with cooking spray.

⁘ In a soup pot over low heat, melt butter. Add marshmallows and stir until completely melted. Remove from heat and stir in cereal until evenly coated. Spoon mixture into Lid-It and press down with spatula. Let cool for 30 minutes. Trim edges and cut into 2-inch squares. Place squares on a wire rack and set aside.

⁘ In a medium microwave-safe bowl, combine caramels and heavy cream. Microwave for 60 to 90 seconds (depending on the wattage of your microwave) or until melted and smooth, stirring occasionally. Drizzle caramel over each square and top with a pecan placed diagonally in center of square. Allow to cool slightly.

⁘ Meanwhile, in a small microwave-safe bowl, combine chocolate chips and shortening; microwave for 60 to 90 seconds or until melted and smooth, stirring occasionally. Drizzle chocolate over top of each square. Let sit until chocolate hardens. Serve at room temperature.

TARA'S TIP: These make a great holiday gift—especially if you gift the Lid-It along with the treats! Talk about an easy way to put a smile on someone's face.

Anytime Ambrosia

This recipe is a tradition. I mean, whether you eat it as a side dish or as a dessert (or both) you can't go wrong. Some people call it "fluff," others call it "Watergate salad," while my family knew it as "ambrosia." At the end of the day, it's all the same deliciousness. And whether you dress this up for Easter, like I did here, or you serve it at a picnic, it's perfect anytime.

Serves: 10 to 12   Prep Time: 10 min   Cook Time: 5 min   Chill Time: 60 min

2 eggs, lightly beaten

¼ cup white vinegar

¼ cup sugar

2 tablespoons butter, softened

1 (8-ounce) container frozen whipped topping, thawed

1 (10-ounce) jar maraschino cherries, drained and cut in half

1 (20-ounce) can pineapple chunks, drained

1 (15-ounce) can mandarin oranges, drained

2 cups miniature marshmallows

½ cup flaked coconut

⁂ Place eggs in the top of a double boiler or in a heatproof bowl over a saucepan of simmering water; simmer over medium-low heat. Add vinegar and sugar and stir constantly for 5 to 7 minutes or until the mixture is slightly thickened and smooth. Remove from heat, stir in butter, and let cool.

⁂ Pour mixture into a large serving bowl. Fold in whipped topping until well combined, then fold in cherries, pineapple, oranges, marshmallows, and coconut.

⁂ Cover and chill for 1 hour or until ready to serve.

TARA'S TIP: I love dressing up my ambrosia for the holidays! For Christmas I serve it up in one of my festive holiday bowls and garnish it with Christmas-shaped marshmallows and for Valentine's Day, I serve this in individual ramekins and top each with a whimsical conversation heart.

Candy Cane Marshmallow Dippers

Add an extra dose of cute to your holidays with these fun and easy marshmallow dippers. They make great gifts (wrap them in cellophane) and look amazing on a holiday dessert table. My favorite way to enjoy them is with a mug of steamin' hot chocolate. (Check out how the candy cane hooks onto the side of the mug!) These are great for kids too—they can help make them and they'll love watching them dissolve into the hot chocolate!

Makes: 6　　　　**Prep Time: 10 min**　　　　**Chill Time: 5 min**

6 mini or large candy canes, unwrapped

6 jumbo marshmallows

½ cup semi-sweet chocolate chips

1 teaspoon vegetable shortening

Assorted sprinkles and decorating candies, as desired

- Line a baking sheet with wax paper. Insert a candy cane into the center of each marshmallow (as shown) and set aside.

- In a medium microwave-safe bowl, combine chocolate chips and shortening; microwave for 60 seconds, stir, and continue to heat in 10 second intervals until chocolate is melted and mixture is smooth. Let cool slightly.

- Dip marshmallows halfway in chocolate, letting excess drip off. Immediately sprinkle chocolate with sprinkles or decorating candies, as desired, and place on wax paper. Allow chocolate to harden at room temperature. If you're in a rush, refrigerate for 10 minutes. Store at room temperature.

> TARA'S TIP: I've got the perfect hot chocolate recipe to go with these. To make it, in a large saucepan, combine ½ cup cocoa powder, ¾ cup sugar, and ¼ teaspoon salt. After mixing that together, gradually stir in 2 cups warm water and let that simmer over medium heat for about 6 minutes or until all the sugar has melted. Stir in 4 cups half-and-half and heat just until it's hot, but not to the point that it comes to a boil. Then it's ready to pour into your favorite temp-tations mugs.

Million Dollar Brownies

Everybody has their go-to brownies, and for many of you that might even be the brownies that come from a box. I'm not saying to give those up, I'm just asking you to trust me on this one and give these a try. Why? Because these might be the most decadent and most satisfying brownies you've ever tasted. You deserve them. Your kids deserve them. The stranger you said hello to yesterday deserves them. They're that good.

Makes: 15 to 18   **Prep Time: 10 min**   **Cook Time: 40 min**

2 sticks butter, melted

¾ cup unsweetened cocoa powder

2 cups sugar

4 eggs

1 cup all-purpose flour

2 teaspoons vanilla extract

½ teaspoon salt

2 cups (12 ounces) dark chocolate chips

¼ cup real bacon pieces (optional)

:: Preheat oven to 350 degrees. Coat a 13- x 9-inch baking dish with cooking spray.

:: In a large bowl, combine butter and cocoa; stir until well blended. Add sugar; mix well. Add eggs, one at a time, beating well after each addition. Add flour, vanilla, and salt; stir until just combined. Stir in chocolate chips. Spread batter in baking dish and sprinkle top with bacon pieces, if desired.

:: Bake for about 40 minutes or until a toothpick inserted in center comes out clean. Let cool, then cut into squares. Store in refrigerator until ready to serve.

❖recipes in alphabetical order❖

✦recipes in alphabetical order✦

✤ recipes by category ✤

❖ recipes by category ❖

❖ recipes by category ❖

❖ recipes by category ❖